MW00719045

"*Fire in the House* is a book for the body of Christ. It will help you recover the fire and passion in leadership. Read it, blow on the ashes of your burn out, and break into flames as the Holy Spirit speaks to you."
—*Dr. Samuel R. Chand, President Beulah Heights Bible College*

"It's obvious that what Bishop Greenwood has to say in *Fire in the House* comes straight from the gut of someone who has walked as a visionary, yet remains a pioneer for all leaders. This riveting revelation will rekindle the fire that God desires to burn within us all."
—*Will Hardy, founder and CEO, The Remnant Ministries, Inc.*

"*Fire in the House* is a rare treasure of godly wisdom, totally scriptural and inspired by the Holy Spirit. I recommend that this book be read by pastors, evangelists, prophets, teachers, and all lay people who truly love the Lord. Bishop Greenwood has certainly penned valuable information that will energize and inspire the body of Christ to keep the *Fire in the House*."
—*Apostle Thomas H. Vinson, founder and Senior Pastor, Highpoint Christian Tabernacle*

"I've known Bishop Greenwood for a number of years. When I read *Fire in the House*, I saw his passion for ministry and leaders for the 21st century. I highly recommend this book to leaders with struggles and questions as they serve the kingdom. After reading it, they will share a common appreciation as myself for Bishop Greenwood's hard work and encouragement."
—*Bishop Nathan J. Anderson, Presiding Prelate, War Fellowship Ministries, Inc.*

"*Fire in the House* will truly set a blaze in your life. God has given him eyes like fire to truly penetrate our insight. Through the power of the Holy Spirit, this book will enlighten the eyes of your understanding. *Fire in the House* will encourage you to develop a closer relationship with the Lord and ignite you to be consumed by the zeal of God."

—*Apostle H.L. Horton, The Day Star Tabernacle International*

To
Sharon

Thank you!

FIRE IN THE HOUSE

Bishop R. E. Greenwood

Release The fire !

R. Greenwood

(Heb 12:29)

Gazelle
P R E S S

Fire in the House by Bishop Raymond E. Greenwood
©Copyright 2006 – Bishop Raymond E. Greenwood

Bible quotes are from the the King James Version of the Bible unless otherwise stated. Bible verses marked TLB are taken from *The Living Bible* copyright ©1971. Used by permission of Tyndale House Publishers, Inc., Wheaton, Illinois 60189. All rights reserved.

Printed in the U.S.
For worldwide distribution.

ISBN 1-58169-227-7

Gazelle Press
P.O. Box 191540
Mobile AL 36619

Table of Contents

Dedication

I would like to take this time to dedicate this book to some wonderful people:

To Dr. Percy Carter of Trinity Bible College, who believed in my writing when I didn't know how to believe in myself. Sir, sleep on in the bosom of our Lord.

To my wife Marion, who never stopped encouraging me to follow my dream. Honey, I love you more!

To my darlings, Darion and Christina, who make every day a blessed day.

To my mom and Dad, Frank and Edna Greenwood, who have already crossed over the Jordan to be with the Lord. You gave me life and love; this one is for you. I miss you!

To Ray, your music is the reason God put you on this earth; share it!

To my apostolic father, T.D. Jakes. I love you, sir, you changed my life, and I'm grateful.

To everyone who reads this book, be encouraged, there is hope—His name is Jesus. Life up your head; our heavenly Father loves you.

Acknowledgments

First, to my Lord and Savior, Jesus Christ. Thank You, Lord, for imparting Your wisdom into my spirit. Without You, this book would never have happened.

To Natile, you brought so much wisdom, joy, and insight to this project. Thank you.

To Angel, FJD—the anointing on your life is so out of this world. Thank you for your friendship, love, and loyalty.

Will—Brother, I love you. You are the man!

Thank you Brian and the Gazelle Press staff for your wonderful cover. God used you to see inside my spirit.

To the Warren P. Sewell Foundation—Thank you for believing in me and for your generous contribution to this project.

To Kathy, you took my project to the next level. Thank you for enhancing my ideas.

To Roslyn and Diane—the best sisters a brother could have. And to my friends Elder Spencer and Lady Stephanie—you are supreme!

To my brother Rick—I'm glad God gave you to me. To all my family—thank you for your untiring support.

Finally to Elder Tracey—you are a true armor bearer and friend. I shall never forget your unflinching support.

Thank you to all. I love you.

Introduction

Day by day, life has a way of revealing insight when you least expect it. One day, as I was waiting in the doctor's office for my annual checkup, I noticed that a few new paintings had been placed on the office wall. As I glanced at each picture, admiring the different scenes, I began reflecting on various thoughts as they entered my mind. One picture, however, grabbed my attention. It was entitled *Fan Into Flame—The Gift of God* by Thomas Blackshear II. It was a painting of five men standing and praying to God as He seemingly hovered over them. They were from different ethnic backgrounds and varied in age from one another. One of the men had no hair and was well seasoned. One was an Indian and was peacefully looking upward. Another had long hair and appeared to be an outdoorsman. One was tall and scholarly. The fifth man I noticed was rustic in looks and seemed to have had a rough life. However, what caught my eye was that they all had a bright gentle flame emanating from their chests. The flames appeared to be alive and reaching for the sky. As I looked, I believed that their individual prayers were permitting God to strengthen them in their life situations and impart to them divine instructions and wisdom for the responsibilities He had given them.

It suddenly dawned on me that I, too, had felt the passion of God burning within me when God had summoned me to be a voice for Him. However, somehow during my life's journey, I had lost something. The Son was no longer burning within me. My fire did not seem as bright, and my conviction was not as certain as it once had been. What had happened? Where was my flame of passion? This book will help you understand and overcome the struggle of losing your passion in life. As you search the scriptures, you will find someone with whom you can identify. Moses, the Old Testament leader of God's people, was responsible for a nation of people. As you begin to study his life, you will see many similarities to your life. He was born at a time when a household needed life. So were many of you. He was raised to believe there was nothing he could not conquer if he put his mind to it. Is this you?

Then, at a time in his life when he thought he had a handle on who and what he was, he discovered that the facts of the matter were not a matter of the facts. The wind of passion was taken from beneath his wings of purpose. Let me invite you to come with me on a walk through the birth, life, flight, and return in the life of Moses. Together, let us see how he regained the passion and fire for his vocation. This book will allow you to look through his eyes and walk in his shoes. You, too, can make a comeback from any situation!

This book was written to help those who have lost their passion for ministry and life. *Fire in the House* will help you regain it and live life as God intended it to be lived—with joy and a genuine love and reliance on Him.

Raymond Edward Greenwood
Prelate over HigherGround Christian Cathedral

Foreword

My first encounter with Bishop Raymond Greenwood was a "God encounter." Introduced by a mutual friend, we spiritually connected immediately because we have the same heavenly Father. Both Bishop and I felt the presence of God in our divine appointment. Since that meeting, we have been friends—dear friends in Christ. I have experienced many times of refreshing in this man's presence. He is truly a man of God.

It is indeed a great pleasure for me to write this foreword. I know that the message that Bishop Greenwood has written within these pages is inspired because he is an inspiration himself! I admire his faith and respect the work that God has called him to do.

FIRE IN THE HOUSE is an explosion of information for you the reader to digest and apply to your life. God is calling for His people—radical people—to take a godly stand. Now is the time to act. Today is the day of salvation. It is time to get up and go. Your house is on fire!

Bishop Greenwood's powerful message is to the world. He is sounding an alarm to those who need to hear the warning—revival is at hand.

God is moving by His Spirit all over the world with signs and wonders of His glory. No longer is your world just the concerns in your house, your church, or your street; but as a person of faith, your calling to minister is now a global calling. The world is crying out for the return of the Lord Jesus Christ. We are on high alert—the house is on fire! This fire cannot be contained. It is the fire of the Lord. The message is clear.

Bishop Greenwood's ministry spans the continents of

Europe. Often he is called to lead crusades for weeks. He answers this call with love and devotion to God.

FIRE IN THE HOUSE is a book for everyone. I recommend that you give this book to those that God has placed under your care—the people you mentor. This book of revelation will cause many to come closer to the Lord. It will also inspire others to seek healing and counsel. Many will find their "purpose for God" through the pages of this book.

Whether you are a seeker, a new believer, or a committed Christian, *FIRE IN THE HOUSE* is for you! Allow God to speak through these pages a message of hope urgency and redemption. After all, when the house is on fire, you must move quickly!

Ann Platz
Minister, Author, Speaker and Designer
Atlanta, Georgia

Preface

Then I said, I will not mention him, nor speak any more in his name. Nevertheless, his word was in mine heart as a burning fire shut up in my bones, and I was weary with forbearing. I could not stay (Jer. 20:9).

We live in a society where morality is ever-changing; what was deemed wrong yesterday is somehow all right today. However, as Christians, we are to live by a standard that exemplifies the Christian faith. Our very posture should leave no room to question the difference between the validity of our faith and the foolishness of this world's system. We find this standard inside the Word of God, and we must follow it in order to experience the fullness of God in our lives. For there to be any level of success while operating in the ministry, there must be a passionate burning within us and a yearning for the heart of God that urges us to follow His will, no matter what the cost. Is there a fire in your "house" that stirs your desire for a more intimate, effective walk with the Father? Remember, fire, which is symbolic of the Holy Spirit, must be a resident in you if you are to experience effectiveness in ministry.

Gift, Present, Release: These are three areas of love that are given from our heavenly Father to us. When the Lord chooses us, He does three things for us: He gifts us; He presents himself to us; He releases himself through us in order that we may truly possess His fire for His house, His people, and His world. We must have the spirit of God and a heart after God that causes us to give priority to doing His will. It is just like a loving God to command us to do a thing, then equip us with the tools we need to accomplish the task, because God's gifts present release. Wow!

> *For the Word of God is quick, and powerful, and sharper than any two edged sword, piercing even to the dividing asunder of soul and spirit, and of the joints and marrow, and is a discerner of the thoughts and intents of the heart* (Heb. 4:12).

I am writing this book because my heart has been burdened with the lack of genuineness in many ministries today. Too often, the superficial message that says, "The Lord will make a way somehow," sings from the lips of religious puppeteers, who seem to stand in line for applause and praise for their song. The Lord is calling us to ministry, not monopolies, to power, not position, to grace not greed.

Have we as preachers sold our birthright for a bowl of pottage called popularity because of our moral indifference, our fear of offending our members, or our willingness to look the other way? There is a mandate given to every man, woman, and child who follows Christ, to proclaim the Word of the Lord in season and out of season—the times when men accept you and the times when men reject you. If God is not pleased, then it doesn't matter, anyway. Would it be wise to sacrifice our conscience at the altar of public opinion? No!

Furthermore, we cannot give into the message of mediocrity, and we can no longer follow a hear-no-evil, speak-no-evil, see-no-evil approach to ministry. (You know, the don't-ask-don't-tell approach.) The gospel message burns with cleansing fire. If the Gospel is to be life-changing and effective, then it must be proclaimed with the fires of passionate conviction and absolute faith and with reliance upon His Spirit and power and His Holiness.

The following are some points to ponder as you deal with the passion and conviction of your calling:

Points of Peace to Practice

1. Realize your greatness in God.
2. God's promises are yours by faith.
3. Get a vision from God and work it.
4. Go forth knowing the Lord is with you.
5. Claim confidence in Christ.
6. The Word shall not depart from you.
7. Go now and possess the land!

The important thing is this: To be ready at any moment to sacrifice what we are for what we could become.

—Charles Dubois

Chapter 1

Fire Anyone?

The purpose of the Church is to lift up Christ through the power of the Holy Spirit, who indwells His people. As we read in the book of Acts, the Holy Spirit appeared as tongues of fire to the believers in the Upper Room. As a result of that encounter, their lives were transformed, and authority was imparted to them. They were empowered by the Spirit to serve and preach an anointed message that turned their world upside down (Acts 17:6).

Just as the fire of God, which is evident in the Holy Ghost, illuminated and transformed the lives of early believers, so, too, that same fire is available for us today and must be appropriated if we are to significantly impact our world for Christ. The Spirit will bring light to our lives, warm (comfort) our hearts, purge us from our wrongs, and purify us wholly. Many church folks have sought the spotlight for man's approval, yet they have circumvented the illumination of a holy fire that is provided just for Christians! They have accepted counterfeit flames, which have caused them to become burned-out and burdened with the hurt and pain of false shepherds who ignited them with strange, unholy fire.

The cunning behavior of some leaders leads us to believe that we can have legitimate results with counterfeit objectives. It may look like, sound like, and glow like, fire—but it is not! Have you ever asked yourself, "Am I being played?" Who is getting the glory here? People have seen the show, now it is time for them to see the Savior. We need transforming Holy Ghost power around us as Moses experienced on Mt Sinai, and the disciples experienced in the Upper Room. We need it in us with the intensity that Jeremiah had. Remember, he said it felt like fire shut up in his bones! Can you recall the times when you said you felt the stirring of God in your life? Who stole the innocence of your anointing? The purpose of this question is not to draw you backwards but to show you that it is time for you to move forward.

The symbol of fire or flames is a representation of the presence of God, for our God is an all-consuming fire. With it, He engulfs us with His presence, which is His wondrous power. The Lord will give His fire to all who earnestly desire it (John 15:26).

Becoming an Instrument

The key to being an instrument that will help change others is for us to first experience the miracle of change ourselves. For example, a pastor who is plagued by pornography, a secretary who is seduced by sex, or a church deacon who is carried away by his own lust for a seductress are not going to be used fully by God in the lives of others. Deliverance can, and has, come for those who were mired in these sins and saw them as impossible strongholds for them to break. Your enemy, the devil, wants you to believe that areas like these are insurmountable. Those who have been delivered from such strongholds can rise up and become instrumental in the deliverance of other impulse-driven children of God.

Our change comes with knowing God as our Savior and Deliverer. Some people like to experiment in an attempt to know God on various levels. For example, some believe their intellect will suffice as a means to know God, but He wants to offer us more than an intellectual interpretation of Himself. He is more than a concept or creative idea concocted by the human mind. Intellect plus creativity divided by experimentation does not equal a real relationship.

Intellectual information about God produces nothing spiritual on its own. Knowledge about the heavenly Father is needful, but if it does not bring transformation to your life and your person, then it is good for nothing. To truly know God requires a lifetime of communion with Him. To know God is to experience Him. Just as fire brings about major changes to whatever it touches, an experience with the all-consuming power of the Holy Ghost will transform you from defeat to victory and bring about the fullness of joy in your life. Soon thereafter, you can help others experience the same transformation.

When the cry of our heart is truly, "Lord, change us!" He, in turn, sends fire. Sometimes He sends fire above us . . . not to cover us, but to correct us. Sometimes He sends fire around us . . . not to warm us, but to cover us. Sometimes He sends fire upon us . . . not to burn us, but to bless us. The way that you know there has been a fire is by the evidence left be-hind—for example, the warm coals that glow for a long time afterward or the ashes that reveal an object has been forever altered.

The fire that God brings into our lives leaves us forever changed when we submit to it. It works in us to ensure that we are freed from our former self and can have a new peace of mind and confidence that will prepare us for the work of the ministry.

God's Glory

When Moses was on Mt Sinai, the Lord used a burning bush to gain his attention. Can you imagine the mesmerizing colors and unusual brightness of light that caught his eyes, stopped him in his tracks, and drew him closer because he could no longer stand still? What kind of fire had such characteristics, yet did not consume its object?

What was unusual about this particular bush was not just that it was burning. As a herdsman, Moses had, undoubtedly, seen bushes burning before. What made this incident unusual was that the bush was engulfed in flames, yet it was not con-sumed. When Moses "turned aside . . . to see this great sight" (Exodus 3:1-3), the Lord seized the opportunity to speak to him from the midst of the flames.

At first glance, the fire looked to be no different than the many campfires he had seen. Yet, as Moses peered into the flames like an insect drawn to a porch light on a hot summer night, they seemed to call to him. Moses was being summoned for service to the King.

There is a morbid fascination, an unexplained magnetism,

that draws people whenever there is a blazing fire. The Lord, who knows our nature, shows us in this story that He certainly knew Moses and employed what surely would gain Moses' undivided attention. Turning aside initially to see, nevertheless, he remained so that he could hear and accept the Lord's call.

Just as God called to Moses long ago, so, too, today He still calls us out of darkness into His marvelous light. Just as God used a bush to gain Moses' attention, God also has a Mt. Sinai for you. It could be in a back alley or on a lonely corner or in a box underneath a bridge where you have been living, forgotten. God will use any means necessary to call you out of sub-living situations and place you on the glorious path that He has prepared for you.

Many years ago, a pastor friend of mine told me a story about an indigent man. One day this man was in a back alley, full of gloom and pity. Out of desperation he fell to his knees, covered his face with his hands, and cried out, "God, why am I here?" After sobbing awhile, he felt the urge to look up, and in the midst of the broken bottles and the foul odors of urine and rotting trash, he saw a rose growing up from a crack in the concrete. Springtime had come to interrupt his personal winter. At that moment, the sun shone brightly from above, spotlighting the glory of the rose. The man looked up and asked, "What is something so beautiful doing in a forsaken place like this?" God tenderly responded, "So that you could see it and have hope." Even in the worst times of our lives, the Lord can use a person, a place, a rose, yes, even a bush to call us from despair to destiny.

He will convict us by the power of His Spirit that burns within our hearts. If we are always faithful to follow His prompting, we will be drawn, discovered, delivered, and directed by Him every time. The fire of God will draw us to relate to Him—to be renewed and to receive revelation about Him.

There is a reality in the fire of God that cannot be denied. Even though Moses was on the run and in hiding because of his past, the Lord knew how and when to approach him. Today, the Lord still has a way of finding His children, even on the backside of a mountain of circumstances.

When people have given up on us, the Lord longs to restore us to a right relationship with Him. To position us to receive His wooing and allow ourselves to be found, God must first provoke us to action. Often, past unresolved issues cause us to go AWOL from friends, family, and even God. We run away attempting to leave everything behind and hope that people will forget what we have been and done. God understands the wrestling in our spirits. He is concerned with the pain of rejection that causes us to abandon all that we know and hold dear and to run into the wilderness. Even at our worst, God loves us unconditionally and offers us restoration. He will find us, fetch us, and fix us, even on the backside of the mountain. The fire of God will give us renewal and restoration. The Lord can even change the rules of nature to summon and reclaim one of His children. The Bible says,

> *Trust in the Lord with all thine heart and lean not unto thine own understanding in all thy ways acknowledge him and he shall direct thy path* (Prov. 3:5-6).

God wants to make us whole. Wholeness is the key to our maturity. It is the completion of our spirits that gives us stability and peace as we follow Him.

Counterfeit Connections

In order to find that wholeness they so desperately need, people seek the Lord in many ways. Some people seek Him through psychic phenomena or other counterfeit means. Any path to God other than the one He has set for us results in pain and loss. Imagine driving all day across the countryside thinking that you have taken a great shortcut, only to have the road dead-end before you, forcing you to turn around, backtrack, and start all over, causing you to lose much time and effort in the process.

All that futile effort! Look at King Saul, who thought he could take a shortcut and found himself rejected because of his disobedience. Because he could no longer discern God's voice, he consulted the witch of Endor for answers.

This is a perfect example of a counterfeit connection. Today, there are "900" numbers, for example, featuring psychics who offer quick links to answers for our lives. They are today's fortunetellers who attract the desperate and gullible and entice them to surrender to counterfeit solutions and predictions. The carrot before our noses is their quick, direct answer. Beware of psychics who would press you to surrender your life to their "answers."

God will not violate His principles to please anyone—not even a king! God does not chase us; He calls us. God gives us free will to choose whether or not we will respond. However, He will direct us if we allow Him to do so, and His Word will inspire us to take our place in Him. If we obey His voice and honor His calling, then we will have an unlimited capacity for greatness. The day we hear His voice, let us not harden our hearts!

Opening Challenge
THE ALPHA

Alerting—The Facts

The enemy wants you to become ensnared in the frustrations of life. However, when you realize whose you are, a real peace will come to you. Remember, you are complete in Him. All you need is in Him. Discover your self-worth and realize the unlimited capacity that is at your disposal. When you're out of practice, things somehow feel out of sync. Many things can happen to interrupt forward progress. Depression or an extended absence due to illness can knock you right out of the game. I've quickly learned that falling is part of the process. The key is to get back up when you fall.

I recently went horseback riding. I hadn't ridden a horse in years, so I was somewhat apprehensive about it. I've gained a few pounds since my last ride, so mounting the horse was not as easy as I had thought it would be. And wouldn't you know it, I fell right off and hit the dirt (ouch). Nevertheless, I was determined to get back on that horse, and I did. Many people, however, quit when they fall, never to try again. Even a briefly intended pause can turn into a permanent situation if it is not ended quickly. Getting back in the saddle is not without its challenges. However, if you stay out of the saddle too long, it's quite possible you will never want to try again. God says "Child, it's not over." So try it once more.

Declaring—Your Role

I hear you saying, "I've tried again and failed again. What do I do next? I've fallen, and I can't get up." When you fall enough times, it can be frustrating, to say the least. But like the fairy tale goes, you must keep kissing that frog until you find your princess. Make up your mind to succeed. You'll win if you don't quit.

Activating—What Will You Do Now?

Wholeness is the key to maturity. This means having a right mind, a clean heart, and honest motives. Make this declaration with me: "Success in my life is not an option, but a benefit. No matter how hard or how fierce the battle, victory belongs to me and my house."

The angel of the Lord encamps around them that fear Him and delivers them (Psalms 34:7).

Chapter 2

Tanners

But the Lord said unto Samuel, look not on his countenance, or on the height of his stature; because I have refused him: for the Lord seethes not as men seethe; for man looketh on the outward appearance, but the Lord looketh on the heart (1 Samuel 16:7).

What Is God Looking For?

When God looks for a man, His requirements are different from ours. God looks at different criteria to qualify His candidate. God told Samuel, the prophet, that He was not concerned with a man's physical make up but rather the inward qualities required for leadership. A person must have more than surface beauty to be used by God. Worldly individuals tend to judge a person based on their conception of what beauty is. The diet and fitness industry makes billions of dollars annually as people strive in vain to achieve what the public perceives as the perfect body. Even Christians can be caught up in the quest for physical perfection and lose sight of the fundamental truth that God does not look at man's outward appearance but at his heart. God sees past the facade of muscle and makeup to peer into our inward parts and see our spirit in the manner a radiology technician views an X-ray negative. His view of us is never clouded by what we have on or what great bodies we have built. God sees and knows us as we are; nothing is hidden from His sight. He is never confused about who or what we are because He looks past our reputation. No matter what age or stage we happen to be in, we are always exposed to the Creator of the universe. The Lord sees not as men see because God reveals the heart of us all.

As I have walked in the parks of Atlanta, I have seen many people trying to change their outward appearance by basking in the sun. They find a space on the limited grass that a metropolis such as Atlanta offers, spread their blankets, and lay for hours. Others do so on beaches, their lawns, or on rooftops, or they use lotions, creams, and oils in search of the perfect tan. I call them "tanners" and use them as an example of the way people strive mightily to change and enhance their appearance while ignoring the most significant part of themselves—their inner parts, which is where their spirit lives.

But, the tanners want only an outside change. They lay motionless in the sun as though to say, "Let me have it!" Through this, they are hoping that the sun will transform them into that perfect physical image. Others are willing to pay for the use of a tanning bed in a salon, wanting a quicker fix. While many people do obtain the perfect tan, their spirits are crying out for restoration. Unfortunately, they ignore these cries and die a silent death from the inside out.

Like these tanners, many Christians have adopted a level of Christian culture in which they look, act, and talk like Christians yet are content to wade in the shallow end of things, unwilling to allow the Holy Spirit to truly change them on the inside. But if He's allowed entrance, God reaches to our innermost parts to challenge us to change. God is calling for commitment from His people. We must be willing to leave the shallows and our comfort zone and launch out into the deep.

People today are infatuated with change. Some of us change our hair color, for example, or use different colored contacts to have a different eye color because we want to change outwardly. Others resort to cosmetic surgery in an attempt to change, or to keep, what they have worked so hard to get. Eventually we become satisfied that others have forgotten what we used to look like, and we have accomplished acceptance. Perhaps that is not always the intent, but that is certainly the result. However, if you attempt to change only outwardly, then pride and vanity become your colleagues.

Some tanners may take their quest for physical perfection to the next level and embark on a planned program of proper nutrition, diet, and exercise. They recognize that in order to attain a lasting physical beauty, it must be supported by inward modification as well. A fit body that is supported by good nutrition will tend to look and feel better for a longer period of time than one that subsists on constant junk food, no matter how good the tan may be on the outside.

Like these individuals, some Christians long for the presence, power, and purpose of God to be manifested in their lives, and they, too, embark on a quest for the next level. They submit themselves to God, allowing Him to change their hearts, thoughts, and motives, knowing that righteousness begins on the inside and is then manifested on the outside. Knowing they cannot swim alone, they have launched out into the deep, keeping their eyes on Jesus and trusting that He will keep them afloat. This is the type of person God can, and will, use.

We must allow the Lord to change us inwardly so that we become what He wants us to be. Look again at the allegory of the tanner. The world says that if you lay in the sun long enough, you will become the perfect color. However, what the world fails to tell you is that the effect of the tan is temporary, because after the summer is over, so is the tan. Our enemy, the devil, can offer only temporary gratification.

Like a tan, the pleasures and benefits of sin are only temporary. Like getting too much sun and causing permanent damage to the skin, buying into the devil's counterfeit benefits causes lasting pain and loss that only the transforming power of the Holy Spirit can heal. We cannot be the source of our own salvation and significance. The power to change inside comes from an inward working of the Holy Spirit. He knows what we need and will not hurt us in the process. The Word may cut us, but it also heals us.

The longer we are exposed to the Holy Spirit, the more we realize how much we continually need Him. Stresses of the world cause us to feel anxious about things that we should place in God's hands while God-given direction curbs the instinct to follow paths that are not in His will. The struggles of life cause us to focus on our immediate needs, but the Lord wants us to depend on the Holy Spirit to direct us into all truth that will sustain us throughout our lives. The Lord wants us to experience abundant life on His terms. Understanding

God is a faith issue. We will understand the Lord only to the degree that we are in covenant relationship with Him. We cannot continue to treat God as if He were a blessing machine, a genie of sorts. Rub Him with enough vigor and He will grant three wishes—No! That is not the way.

We should not follow the Lord just because He is good to us. We should follow and serve Him solely because He is God. If we reduce God to a blessing god, we miss the fact that He is all-knowing (omniscient), all-powerful (omnipotent), and present everywhere at once (omnipresent). We need to reach beyond the blessing and latch onto the One who blesses.

We need to have fellowship with God. It is only then that we will have communion with Him and always be blessed. Our relationship with God should not diminish because of the circumstances in our lives. If it does, we need to repent and seek His face, for we have probably never truly known Him. A true knowledge of God brings about a love and fervor that will sustain us through the worst that life offers and imparts a deep, settled peace even in the midst of the sorrows and frustrations that temporarily overtake us.

God will supersede all circumstances, powers, and principalities. The dilemma that sometimes overwhelms us is how to trust God when the circumstances do not reveal His presence or preeminence. Fellowshiping with the Lord means following Him through the times when we cannot make sense of the events or are not being understood by others. We must value His direction because He knows the way. When the going gets rough, God will give us strength to continue on.

Challenge 2
JEHOVAH ADONAI—
THE LORD OUR SOVEREIGN

Alerting—The Facts

We are what we eat. We are titillated by an elegant place setting in a fine restaurant. The china and stemware are gleaming. We sit down in anticipation of what is about to be served. The waiter brings our plate on a silver platter covered with a silver lid. As he uncovers it, we are repulsed at what is underneath—rotting, uncooked, maggot-filled food. Would you eat it? Probably not. However, how many times have we spiritually partaken of what appeared to be okay, but in reality was not. We are what we eat. Think about it.

Write down your activities for one day: everything you eat spiritually, everyone you see, what you watch on TV, and what you read. Our appetites are symptomatic of the problems on the inside of us. We need to let God prepare our plates. Do you realize most of us haven't spent 15 minutes in the Word or in prayer during an entire week? You are hereby challenged to immediately exchange one meal for one chapter in God's Word.

Declaring—Your Role

God says we are treating His house like Wendy's. We've gotten all dressed up and have passed through church service just as we go through a Wendy's drive-through window where the attitude is, "Give it to me quickly. I've got to go!" We come to church and get that bag of food once a week, while we are being entertained but receive no lasting nourishment.

We are underweight and weak spiritually because of a lack of spiritual nourishment. We cannot survive on a daily diet of fast food. This is war! We are seeing it in our homes, our finances, our relationships, our children, and our health. Where can we go but to God?

Activating—What Will You Do Now?

Every week we take care of household maintenance such as washing the dishes, wiping off the kitchen counter, or taking out the trash. It's funny that we are more faithful about that kind of maintenance than we are about our spiritual maintenance.

Let's repent and become passionate for God and let Him examine us—not to beat ourselves to death, or to start some fake list of humility, but to make a real assessment of where we are. God says that we are fearfully and wonderfully made in His image and likeness. The question to ask ourselves is, What do I need to surrender? Do we daily ask God how we can please Him? To tell you the truth, some days, I have to do it hourly. To really trust God, we have to give up any appetite, behavior, attitude, or part of ourselves that we know is displeasing to Him. Do you read the Word faithfully? Sometimes we do the things that look right, but we do not allow God to touch us to the core.

Nothing with God is accidental.

Chapter 3

Images

I begged your disciples to cast the demon out, but they couldn't (Luke 9:40 TLB).

Position is our ability to understand who we are in Christ Jesus. Position, then, is not a level of ranking, as in the military, but it is the awareness that God is, and always will be, the author and finisher of our faith. When we truly understand this, we realize that there is no place for competitiveness in the Body of Christ.

Peter understood Jesus. He walked with Him and slept when He slept; they were in covenant. Their common purpose was to please the Father. Peter understood his role in their relationship. Jesus was his Lord and a teacher who guided him through the uncharted areas of life. Peter was the student, willing to die for the man whom he loved as master and friend. Peter believed in Jesus. He spoke plainly to Jesus on the shore of Lake Galilee: " . . . at thy word. Although we've been fishing all night and have caught nothing, nevertheless, I will let down my net" (Luke 5:5). Why? Because he had position, and he understood that Jesus also held a position greater than his own.

Under the inspiration of the Holy Spirit, Peter boldly proclaimed, "Thou art the Christ the son of the living God" (Matt. 16:16). Yet, when fearful and under duress, Peter blurted out to three witnesses in the high priest's courtyard that he never knew Jesus. How could Peter know Jesus so intimately and enjoy such fellowship, yet readily deny Him such a short time later? Peter's plight is also ours because, despite our best intentions, we sometimes lose sight of who Jesus is. When this happens, we start to deny the very One who called us out of darkness into the light. The Bible says, "He came into His own and they received Him not" (John 1:11). To embrace fear is to surrender hope and accept defeat. The Bible says that "God has not given us the spirit of fear but of power, of love and a sound, stable steadfast mind" (2 Tim. 1:7). When we arrest the messes in our lives and surrender to the Holy Spirit, He will, with our permission, transform and transition our lives into the will of the Father, as in the words of the popular hymn:

Have thine own way Lord, have thine own way.
Thou art the potter I am the clay.
Mold me and make me, after thine will
While I am waiting yielded and still.

Let God have control, follow His lead, trust His Word, and release yourself to God. Allow Him to build a strong, sure foundation of faith within you.

A firm foundation is the key to proper development in Christ. Always build upon His foundation. "In all thy ways acknowledge Him and He will direct thy paths" (Proverbs 3:6). To understand your foundation in Christ, mark your beginning in Him by trusting Him.

When we recognize our strengths and weaknesses, it will help us to navigate through uncharted waters. God's provision for us is based on His foundational principles of order, wisdom, prosperity, and government, not our wants and priorities. That is why His strength is made perfect (brought to light) in our weakness. We need the Lord to sustain us.

A great prophet asked, "To whom is the arm of the Lord revealed?" The answer is "To them that understand, the Lord supplies their needs."

It is the Lord who provides, and besides Him, there is no other man, power, or nation that provides as He does. The way in which we view God will determine our level of faith in Him. If we can't trust Jesus, then why relate to Him?

What Is Faith?

Faithfulness is a by-product of having an ongoing, interactive relationship with Him. Faithfulness is not an event in time or just a subject that is taught in Sunday school, but it is a response to a holy call, a response to a holy deposit in our spirit that longs to be released. Faithfulness is not an option; it is the essence of what helps us trust in God. He gives to us, and we respond with faithfulness. How do we respond, with all our finite limitations and imperfections, to an infinite holy God? In our humanness, our expressions to God are manifested as dancing and praising brought forth from our own mouths and our own voices. It is pleasing and acceptable to Him. Our bodies even receive Him in praise. Most of all, we respond to Him with obedience.

Do our disciplines relay how we feel about Him as our Lord and King? In general, do people who observe us and note our relationship (or lack thereof) with God, have a clear picture that we are not ashamed of Him? The world outside can judge how we feel about our Savior only by the actions we present before them. Take for example, the story found in Luke 9:37. A man brought his demon-possessed son to Jesus' disciples, and they could not cure him. The father of the boy made a determination that Jesus had no power because His disciples—His closest followers—demonstrated no power or ability to heal his son. It is easy to understand that he had such an impression because Jesus' followers exuded powerless behavior at a critical time.

The father could not overcome his impression of their powerlessness with faith because he had no relationship with Jesus. He was depending on those who knew Jesus and counting on their connection to the Master to cure his son. Often, unsaved individuals will treat believers as some kind of spiritual junction box that will make a hook-up to Jesus for them. This is true even today. People are still coming to church expecting a power surge from other believers—anybody, somebody—without having a personal relationship with Him. However, our job as Spirit-filled believers is to replicate His life and help others establish an individual connection with Him for themselves. When they have a personal relationship with Jesus, they will learn how to trust Him.

Barriers in responding to the call of Christ come only because the enemy, Satan, wants people to remain unresponsive to His clarion call to deliverance and stay dependent on themselves and not the Lord.

Influences in our lives such as family, friends, associates, surroundings, the media, books, newspapers, literature, and popular culture affect us—sometimes overtly, at other times, subtly. Sometimes the water of our souls becomes muddy with all the confusion, pressure, and deadlines in our lives. It becomes difficult to ascertain what should have the greater impact in our lives and rule our feelings. As God's people, we are more often reactionary than revolutionary. The tendency is to remain traditional in our thinking and to ignore the urging and prodding of the Holy Spirit. Normalcy is the enemy of intervention and has held captive the advancement of man's spirit for centuries. Complacency and remaining comfortable have stunted the spiritual growth of many a person.

It Takes Faith to Follow

Whom shall I send, and who will go for us? Then said I Here am I; send me (Isa. 6:8).

To become strong, faith must be exercised. We need to walk by faith and not by sight. Moving beyond what is seen or felt is the true test of faith. I feel that real faith cannot be shaken or repealed. I do, however, believe that it can be challenged. The Bible says that faith without works is dead. We should know Christ, love Him, and trust in Him. We have to accept God as our Father and leader before faith becomes a reality in our lives. Sometimes we act as though we need the Lord to give us a pep talk regarding our faith. While it does take faith to follow Him, many times we don't follow in faith.

Our relationship with Him is worth the struggle. Faith builds strong character. However, strong faith with strong character is developed through the rough and dry times of life. Even though you have great faith, you will not always get everything you want, but what is more important is that you make the best use of what you are given. The disciples followed Jesus and lived with Him every day. The Bible does not say they wore silk or the softest linen or lived in palaces and enjoyed having their every wish granted to them, but it says their needs were always met, and they never went hungry.

Despite the miracle of divine provision, on many occasions, they seemed unaware of who Jesus really was because they were limited by their finite flesh. As Spirit-filled believers, we even sometimes miss the mark, but the Holy Spirit is still there to lead and guide us. Know this: God still loves us.

His mercies are new each and every morning, and His great faithfulness is beyond our comprehension. Since the Bible reminds us that it is impossible to please God without having faith in Him (Heb. 11:6), I would like to challenge you to take a chance and believe God. Unlike playing the lotto or going to a casino, taking a chance on God will never result in loss.

Following the Lord requires much trust. As you follow God, ask yourself two questions: Do I really trust Him? More important, can He really trust me?

Challenge 3
JEHOVAH SHABOATH—
THE LORD OF HOSTS

Alerting—The Facts

Curves! Sometimes it feels like life is one big curve. We have become accustomed to accepting many things in life, such as bad traffic, rain, snow, taxes, and the common cold. Now I realize, being the astute and perceptive person that you are, that you realize the details in life add up to some significant differences between what you want and what you have.

Have you ever said, "Please fix me, Lord. I give up"? Life is stressful; however, the Lord has the solution for us. If we just surrender our problems to Him, then He will handle our situations and fill the voids in our spirits.

Declaring—Your Role

He is the only wholeness for our brokenness. He knows our skeletons and where the missing pieces are. Sometimes the problem is structural (on the inside). At other times, there is something in a life experience that has weighed down the soul until one becomes accustomed to looking down. It is very difficult to see God, or even to look up, from a stooped position. Nevertheless, by any means necessary, it must be done.

Activating—What Will You Do Now?

One of the many untruths the enemy of our soul (and father of all lies) perpetuates is that God provides us with burdens. While He may allow them, God's purpose is not to break the back of His children. With love, He provides directions for

23

our lives. Some are more difficult than others, and some are less understandable than others, especially if one fails to count God's infinite wisdom into the equation. Nevertheless, He guides us and tells us that we can be transformed by the renewing of our minds. Release yourself to His loving will.

———•◦••◦•———

Patience is accepting a difficult situation without giving God a deadline to remove it.
—Benjamin R. Dejong

Chapter 4

Mine Only Son

And, behold, a man of the company cried out, saying, "Master, I beseech thee, look upon my son: for He is mine only child" (Luke 9:38).

The anguished father of the demon-possessed son wanted more than help, for he was painfully aware how his child's affliction affected his family. In his desperate cry for help, he sought deliverance from the curse of stale, reactionary religion. He wanted a fresh intimacy with God. He knew the God of the old law, but he realized his need for, and longed for, an experience with the new covenant Lord—the Lord of deliverance and restoration. He did not allow the bondage of traditional religion, with all of its limitations and restrictions, to stop him from pursuing the Lord for the restoration of his son and, thus, his entire family. He was not just crying out to God, "Lord, my son needs you!" In essence, he was saying, "Lord, my whole household needs you! I need you! My country needs you! Please release us to become what you have created us to be. By releasing everyone in my family, we will be released, restored, and renewed in our spirits. As the head of my household, I need you right now. I need hope. I need to know who you are, not historically, but personally, not by word of mouth or by what you did for others, but by my own experience." The Lord Jesus responded to his heart's cry: "Sir, all things are possible to him that believe" (Mark 9:23).

It was at that moment that the afflicted boy's father made the faith connection, causing him to go from depletion to affirmation and appreciation. "Lord, I believe! Help thou my unbelief" (Mark 9:24). The Lord will never leave us vulnerable when we come to Him. He will receive us at our place of surrender.

In turn, the boy's father cast tradition aside and, for the first time, he knew Jesus for who He was. Jesus was no longer the Lord of his neighbor. He had become Lord of the neighborhood. The father's expression showed everyone how he felt about Jesus. Deliverance is a powerful restorer of faith. This man was now released from deception and division.

Likewise, in this present hour, the mysteries of God are revealed in His Word and through His person. Through His Word, He reveals His purpose for His people. How does this relate to you? It is time to make a demarcation. Were you once one of those who were dependent on others for a borrowed connection? If so, you, too, can experience deliverance from deception and division. Just cry out to the Lord and say, unashamedly, "Lord, help my unbelief." What is it that motivates Gods people to excellence and fellowship? Is it what He offers us, His salvation, or what He has spoken to us, His promise, that sparks a flame in our hearts? The mysteries of God are only revealed to dwellers—those believers who are occupying until the Lord returns.

Living With Fire

Moses, the "Prince of Egypt," did not grow to young manhood knowing the God of Israel. His god was Ra, the Egyptian god that represented fire. It was on Mount Sinai that the Lord caught Moses' attention by the use of flames, something that Moses knew and understood. Moses had been well schooled in the art of using fire to forge raw metal into pliable utensils. He knew that fire was able to change the very structure of a thing. As a metalworker, Moses knew that fire melted and softened metal, making it pliable. Fire caused it to contour without destroying its innate properties.

Moses further knew that after fire had heated metal, hammering could remove its surface impurities, or dross, thereby creating an instrument that was not only functional but also lovely and strong. In its raw state, metal is not suitable for service. It must be strengthened by fire to be used.

The Intimate Presence of God

God spoke to Moses through the miracle of a burning bush that was not consumed or changed. "Moses, what do you see?" (Exodus 3:3). He saw the fire burning the bush, but the fire was not reacting normally. The bush seemed to be supporting the flame, holding it like a stop sign. And that is exactly what Moses did; he stopped dead in his tracks and turned to see the great mystery. This is where God begins to meet us, too, at that turning point in our spirit. During this encounter on the

mountain, God revealed several things to Moses that I believe
we can benefit from. First, fire REVEALS; it illuminates.
Second, fire CREATES; it provides energy and the capability
for change. Finally, fire INITIATES; it is our genuine source of
motivation.

God went inside of Moses' world to meet him. He ac-
costed him by speaking to him in terms he understood. Out of
the bush, God called him, and he answered. Today, He is still
calling to us in terms each of us can understand: "The day you
hear his voice harden not you heart" (Heb.. 3:15). Why does
God use fire as a manifestation of the Holy Ghost? It lights up,
warms up, purges, and purifies. These are four dimensions in
which I know the Holy Spirit can work for us in our ministry.
Let us examine this phenomenon more closely.

We have discussed the fact that fire reveals; it exposes us
to God. The word revelation derives from the root word reveal, which means "to unveil something or to make plain."
God must be the focal point in our spiritual vision. Moses
needed to see God in the fire because that is where his understanding of salvation was. The fire of the Lord was different
from what Moses was accustomed to because it brought insight, revelation (illumination), and an understanding of
God's perfect, revealed will.

The flame that did not consume illustrated that God was
in control of what happened around him and that He was
greater than just a source of information or an association.
The flames showed that inspiration alone must fuel Moses'
purpose and reason for being from that point onward. No
other agenda was acceptable. The purpose of the bush was not
to give off heat, but to produce vision. We will never see God
until we realize His ways are not our ways and His purposes are

altogether different from our own. When we walk with God, changes will occur. Our cultural views will change. What was once the norm will no longer serve as the precedent for our lives. God's presence has a way of altering the behavior of all things. For instance, in the 10 plagues that He used against Pharaoh, the insect kingdom was drafted into service. The locusts became the air force, the frogs became His navy, and boils became the chemical warfare. God will use whatever He needs to use! God is preeminent, and His creative, preemptive power was illustrated in the bush that burned but did not diminish. All things respond to the perfect will of God.

God Spoke It!

In Genesis, during the creation of this world, God spoke, and birds came forth, and fish began to swim. The sun burst into view, and the stars were hung in place, all in response to the will of God. Moses needed to know that the God of the bush was not only the Lord of the mountain but also of Egypt, Goshen, and even of Pharaoh, himself. All things center on the God of the Universe, the one true God by whom and for whom everything was made. However, God's creative power is not to be experienced without cost to you. Moses was admonished by the Lord to "draw not hither" (Exo. 3:5). He also said, "Put off thy shoes from thy feet, for the ground whereon thou stand is holy ground" (Exo. 3:5). Finally, the fire in the bush reveals God as the initiator of all things.

He is the author and finisher of our faith. He draws us to fellowship and then initiates a hunger for greater intimacy with Him. He stirs up a spirit of faith and faithfulness within us as we reach toward Him. Just as a toddler takes wobbling, hesitant steps in the beginning and soon learns to walk and run, so, too, we become stronger when our faith is exercised as we continue to seek God's face and practice what He teaches us.

Get Up From That Place!

In our yearning and reaching for God, we learn obedience, respect, and reverence for Him, not only as the God who loves us beyond description but also as the one true God who is holy, absolutely sinless, and totally just and righteous. The Lord is calling you to action. He is calling you from the dungeon of your depression and the basement of your broken heart. He wants you to come up from the trauma of your trials. Rise up now from the pain of your abortion or the misery of your miscarriage. He is calling you from Prozac or other antidepressants; Thyroxin, Benzene, GHB, Ecstasy ("X"), pornography, and all the anchors and pacifiers that have held you at bay and allowed the enemy to have his liberty with you. Just as in those old cartoons where the villain tied the damsel to the tracks, making her vulnerable to be run over by the oncoming train, you, too, have been tied to emotional tracks, and it is time for you to rise up from them. Jesus has come to set the captives free, the preacher free, and to free the evangelist and the bishop, too! Whom the Son sets free is free indeed. All who have been called to greatness will have great opposition. Believe it! Don't just stand, or sit, there! Do something! Go somewhere! Be something! Expect something!

Moses needed to see that when God starts a creative work in us and gives us a commission, His purpose is not to use us up, but to show us off as having become more than anyone thought we could be. The flaming bush was Moses' wake-up call from the Lord. Everything that Moses did from that point on showed forth the glory of the Lord. Moses' mountainside encounter with God forever changed his view of the God of Israel. God was no longer a signpost, a figure, a wisp of smoke, or a mythical being. He was revealed as ever abiding and ever initiating. The glory of God was not simply holding a place around Moses, but for the first time, it became a part of him, like a wonderful invasion, unstoppable and all consuming. When Moses returned from his unexpected rendezvous, the glory of the Lord was on him. His countenance shone before all who looked upon him. The Lord longs to impart His glory to us in this way and to set His seal on us for service. God's glory is our covering. It is His sign of approval, and His approval will initiate His glory.

The Majesty of God Revealed

God revealed His majesty when Adam and Eve were created in the garden. His glory clothed them, and nothing else was needed or desired as long as they abided in the center of His will. Just as Satan beguiled Eve with false information, causing both Adam and her to be enticed to step outside of the covering of God's perfect will, so, too, false information and deception today will sometimes prod us to leave the glory of God for other things or lifestyles. In the final analysis, it is His glory and the abiding presence of His Spirit that keep us in check and living inside His will. In order to make it in this life, we need His covering and presence.

He promises us: "Certainly I will be with thee" (Joshua 1:9). We can rest in that abiding promise forever. "For in His presence is the fulness of joy and at his right hand there are pleasures for ever more" (Psalms 16:11). These promises are contingent upon our obedience and willingness to abide in Him.

Just as the Lord gave Moses a sign and an attention-getter, so, too, He is revealing Himself today through His Word and personal experiences that help us form testimonies of His power. How many times have you been in accidents or other mishaps when you knew you should not have made it out alive? God is still speaking, healing, and moving today because He is not just a God of the Old Testament, but He is also a God of the 21st century. He knows what it takes to get your attention, yet you must be willing to turn aside to see what He wants. He will meet you where you are and will always talk to you in a language you can understand. When we have the type of life-changing encounter with God that Moses had on the mountain, we come away from that experience with more than what meets the eye. The Lord will equip the seeker with the spirit of might. Some folks may think Moses came down from that mountain with nothing but a staff and a vision. Not so! The Almighty, El Shaddai, the God who is more than enough, imparted to Moses something that men do not readily see at first glance. God gave him an anointing and authority. Moses was now empowered with the spirit of might to act on the behalf of a mighty God. He can take anyone and equip him or her to become useful. Moses was not eloquent in speech, nor was he a gifted politician or statesman, yet he was anointed for service and equipped to stand before the most powerful earthly ruler of his day. When we read this account of one such servant, we need to consider what might be in our own hands.

Who, me, you ask? Yes you! God can use you, not because you are worthy, popular, or even greatly gifted, but because you are available and willing to be used. Right now, I am going to speak a word to pastors and leaders: Executive officers, never become caught up in the position of who you are and let it dictate what you are. You must always point and lead people to Jesus! Why? Because, believing your own press will never manifest as anything but self-edification and pride and an eventual sorrowful downfall. We must, as Moses did, turn to God and see what He has for us to do. Regardless of where He takes us, we must follow. As a child of God, we need to follow our destiny to wherever it leads us. God does not call us because we are worthy or popular or rich. He calls those who will obey His voice. Obedience is a key to being anointed. Romans 8:30-31 says, "...Whom He did predestinate, He also called: and whom He called, them He also justified [imparts right-standing and authority] and whom He also justified, them He also glorified [reveals His nature and majesty]." If God is for us, who can be against us?

Coincidence or Planned

We are always on the edge of our perception.

And we saw some of the Anak there, descendants of the ancient race of giants, we felt like grass hoppers before them for they were so tall (Num. 13:33 TLB).

This is a report of defeat! Is God's will for your life a fluke or a mishap? Is it planned down to the smallest detail? Does the Lord have a plan for you at all? How do you see yourself? Is your life a series of chance encounters, or does God have it all under control? These questions must be answered if you are to become effective in ministry.

Do we see ourselves as grasshoppers faced with giants in our own lives? "When the wicked rule the people morn, but when the righteous are in authority the people rejoice" (Prov. 29:2). If the righteous God rules and reigns in our lives and imparts His righteousness and authority to us, we have cause to rejoice, not mourn or belittle our circumstances. We are unique to God, so we should never label ourselves based on what we see around us. God is in control.

The 12 spies commissioned by Moses were instructed to scout the land to see what lay before them. Ten of the spies returned with an evil report based on misdirected vision, lack of faith, and inaccurate information. Only two of the 12, Joshua and Caleb, returned with the assurance that the Lord had not lied, and what He promised, He had faithfully delivered. Perception is how we interpret facts. We frequently view the outside world based on our own inner landscape.

Our need of deliverance can be all the weakness Satan needs to be able to feed us erroneous information that can cause us to come away with a false perception based on theory and false conclusions. Incorrect perception can act like an insidious virus that becomes infectious, causing spiritual and moral malaise, immobility, and even death. It will cause us to be separated from truth that imparts life. For example, infection will cause the body to fight against itself, in the same way that a lie, perpetrated by the father of lies, will cause us to fight against the will of God. As a result, we will blame God or someone else for our own inadequacies. God, on the other hand, encourages us to focus our attention not so much on what we see, but rather on who He is—our sustaining provider, the God who is more than enough, the God of covenant who never fails to keep His promises.

Reflection in Rehearsal

The Lord's promises are true, no matter how bleak our circumstances may be. No matter how seemingly impossible our situation is, His promises remain true. It is impossible for our perception to coincide with God's view when we view the world with natural eyes. The 10 spies could view their surroundings with only natural eyes. Joshua and Caleb saw the same surroundings, but they looked through eyes of faith and could boldly proclaim, "Let us go up at once, for we are well able to overcome them and possess the land God has promised us" (Num. 13:30). They knew God would be with them in any situation, even in the face of giant obstacles. They had a relationship with the God of promise and could, therefore, rely directly on His promises. Frequently, our view of ourselves is not the same as God's view of us because He sees what we cannot. God never promised us a life free from challenges, but He did promise to give us a fresh (new) word for our present circumstances.

We cannot follow God while maintaining our perception of His direction. We have to get the heart of God and not be content to keep our own. If we do not, we are doomed to be defeated persons who fall short of their fullest potential. Whose report will we believe? The fire of the Holy Spirit will not let us compromise with mediocrity or settle for the sake of comfort.

We cannot afford to fight among ourselves in an attempt

to decide whose perception is correct. It is a foolish waste of time and energy, and it grieves the Holy Spirit of our living God. Our views will always have a tendency to be faulty. But the Spirit knows what the will of God is. "For we walk by faith and not by sight (2 Cor. 5:7)." Beloved, you can never be less than the God you represent. "Our God is an awesome God— Who can stand beside him?" (Deut. 4:35 paraphrased)

We cannot experience God's will for our lives unless we come into agreement with Him! God is the only true source of strength. Strength can be found in Him and in Him alone. God sees us as blessed, so how do you think we should view ourselves? Ask God to give you a fresh revelation of who you really are in Him. I guarantee you are not a grasshopper!

Challenge 4
JEHOVAH SHAMMA—
THE LORD IS PRESENT

Alerting—The Facts

I have one question for you: Who's your daddy? In a custody battle, great emphasis is placed on who will have custody of the children. The good news is that we belong to God. The bad news is that the anti-father, Satan, doesn't want that arrangement to remain intact. It is his desire to keep us from our rightful Daddy. Take a piece of legal paper and write the devil this little note:

> Dear devil, I'm sorry to be the bearer of bad news, but
> I never belonged to you. I belong to God. Sorry things
> didn't work out. Children are really better off with

their natural parents. I am notifying you that, because of the blood of Jesus, I've been brought back into fellowship with my heavenly Father, where I belong. Through a DNA (Divine Natural Anointing) test, I discovered that you are not my real father. I, hereby, return everything you gave to me as an inheritance: all cancer, all poverty, all lack, all sickness, and death. I won't need them, because my real Daddy will supply all my need according to His riches in glory. He has summoned me to produce good fruit. Your loss is my gain. Yours truly, I'm Delivered.

Declaring—Your Role

When I was a boy, my uncle had a coal furnace in his home. To light the furnace, you had to layer in paper, then wood, and finally coal. You lit the paper first, which lit the wood, which then fired the coal. However, sometimes the coal wouldn't catch on fire. Too many ashes from previous fires kept the coal from catching on fire. Because of the ashes in our lives, some of us aren't as hot as we could be or don't have the effectiveness that we could have. The business of getting rid of ashes is a constant job, but it will keep your spiritual furnace operating at peek performance.

Activating—What Will You Do Now?

Getting it right is not always easy. We stumble along the way, but God will give us wisdom and authority. However, He gave us the power of choice. Choice determines direction and dictates a course of action. Power is determined by source and resource. God is our source. Power means "having the ability to produce." God made you a producer. What are you pro-

ducing? Producers will always dominate consumers. You have
the God-given power within you to make a difference in this
life. Do something with it.

———•••••———

*I declare that peace is not an option
for me but a benefit. No matter how hard, long
or fierce the battle, keeping my mind on
Jesus will keep me in perfect peace.*

Chapter 5

Becoming of Age

Order will come to our lives if we give the Lord His proper reverence and appropriate place within our lives. Part of understanding God's divine order is the realization that He has control over the seasons in our lives. As we pass through these seasons, some will be pleasant and some strenuous, yet our maturing walk with the Lord demonstrates that He is a constant revelator and adjuster of our circumstances.

The story in John 2:6-8 about the wedding in Cana tells of Jesus performing His first miracle—turning water into wine. When Jesus arrived at the feast, most of the wine was gone and the host was about to be embarrassed. I call this lack of wine a type of emptiness. The host and Jesus were close friends, so His mother, family, and Mary appealed to Jesus for help. His answer seemed to refute her request. "Women, what have I to do with thee? Mine hour is not yet come." In other words, He had not planned to enter public ministry at that point and knew if He acceded to her request, His actions would place Him in the public eye. Nevertheless, in faith, she commanded the servants to follow His instructions. We know the rest of the story. Jesus requested that six empty water pots be filled to the brim, and the water became wine. That was authority in action.

Six Empty Pots

Picture six empty water pots sitting against a wall. Like the water pots, we may find ourselves empty and set against the wall. How do you maintain your focus during the times when it seems as though nothing is stirring in, or through, you? Imagine that you once carried weight because you were full of the Spirit, life, and power, but now you are empty because people have taken from you without replacing anything.

Let's go back to the six water pots. The Bible says that there were only a few gallons in each pot—not enough for man to bother with, but just enough for Jesus to use. Are you experiencing the empty feeling of frustration, knowing you were created for a better life? Have you been used and abused by people and left empty and against a wall? Help is on the way! Stand strong and hold on. If you are having a season of dryness or emptiness, God has not forgotten you.

God sees you and will restore what has been taken away. Fill them up is the Master's command! These are words of renewal and provision. When Jesus comes, He will never leave you in an empty state, for He is able to add value to your spirit again. Jesus knew that for us to experience the victorious life, He would have to fill us up with His Spirit.

He makes the same provision for us today that He made

on the day of Pentecost, when believers in the Upper Room were filled with the Spirit and empowered with boldness and authority for service.

Fill them up! For stability, fill them up, for they are vessels ready for use. The Lord does not get caught up in the conflict of choosing which pot to use. As an example, there are six pots, which one do you taste? Which vessel holds the provision? I believe whatever Jesus touches will have provision and whatever He addresses will possess power.

So, it doesn't matter which pot you pick—all of them have been touched by Jesus. Likewise, today He does not look at us and choose us according to who is a good speaker or who has a lovely singing voice. God will use every vessel that is available for His touch.

Jesus Can Fix It!

Regardless of its outward appearance, whether it is brand new or discarded, dirty, and cracked, Jesus is able to repair and renew any vessel to hold His finest provision—His very own Holy Spirit.

The conditions that hold us empty and against the wall do not prevent the Lord from fulfilling His purpose in us. He gives gifts to us. They are His expression of ministry. He releases gifts through us; they are His expression of love to us. He deposits gifts in us; they are the expression of His ownership of us. We belong to the Lord. "We are his people and the sheep of his pasture" (Psalm 100:3).

Walking with God involves more than sharing space with Him. This walk must include acceptance and surrender while following Him. Because He is our leader, we must ardently follow. His direction is key!

We can perceive God's direction only by living closely with Him in every aspect of our lives. His direction is not found with a compass, and, certainly, His divinely inspired will, which can only be breathed on us, is not to be found on any map. It is simply revealed day-by-day via intimate, personal fellowship with Him. Experience is also a key element in walking with God. Determining growth depends on who is judging us and what values are being assessed. Although struggles cause worry and worry brings discontentment, these are often indicators that tension and contentions are eating at us from within.

The only way to grow is to release the struggle into His hands. The growth factor rests in our obeying His will, and not in the size of our accomplishments

Too Much Weight

Guess what? Growth always involves pain. I have not always had a love for exercise, and I am sure a few of you can identify somewhat with me. I just don't like pain. Weight lifting offers many advantages, but there is a down side. I discovered that when I work out in the gym, my body is subjected to tension in an attempt to build muscle and lose fat. With weight lifting, the objective is to stretch muscles beyond their capacity so that they will grow. However, the initial side affect is pain. When you have a good workout, pain will always precede the growth.

With the passage of time, I became more physically fit, and the discomfort was not as great, and the pain was not as severe. So it is with growing in God and maturing in the Spirit. There will be pain as God takes you from one level to the next.

He will move you from what is comfortable to a place that will cause you to stretch beyond what is customary to you. As you move from one comfort zone to another, you will become stronger because of the growth that results when you mature as a Christian. You will be able to bear greater tests and have a deeper anointing as you come to realize that not only are you able to trust God but also that God can trust you, as well.

The Lord's perfect will will always be in conflict with our flesh, but we need to remember that the Lord is not trying to hurt us. Surrendering to God requires us to die to ourselves. This dying, of course, does not entail a physical death; rather, a complete surrender of our will to His. When we have surrendered to Him, we will not react like wind-tossed children to every adverse circumstance.

The Spirit will train the flesh to behave because it is the stronger of the two. In very much the same way that weights will create a well-conditioned athlete, the Word of God can become our trainer. And by obeying the will of the Lord, we unite our spirit to His. Knowing the will of the Lord gives us direction and growth. Psalms 118:8 says, "It is better to trust the Lord than to put confidence in man." The Holy Spirit is the informant of the will of the Lord. He knows the Truth and will help to guide us into all Truth. The Holy Spirit requires us to be willing vessels and committed believers. The Lord then orders our steps.

Do You Have What It Takes to Cross Your Jordan?

Now after the death of Moses the servant of the LORD it came to pass, that the LORD spake unto Joshua the son of Nun, Moses' minister, saying, Moses my servant is dead; now therefore arise, go over this Jordan, thou, and all this people, unto the land which I do give to them, even to the children of Israel. Every place that the sole of your foot shall tread upon, that have I given unto you, as I said unto Moses (Joshua 1:1-3).

This is another question we must all answer. Joshua, the faithful servant, stood alone as a leader. Moses, God's servant, was dead. "Now, therefore arise" (vs.2), said the Lord to Joshua. How those words must have rung in Joshua's ears. Now was the time to draw on all the years of experience and teaching he had received from Moses while working as his assistant. As Moses walked closely with the Lord, Joshua had walked closely with Moses. Although he walked closely with Moses and saw his faults and limitations, Joshua never complained or had a negative word or cause for censure against his leader. He trusted Moses, and Moses trusted him. Now it was time to stand alone and trust God for himself. Moses had crossed the Red Sea, and now it was time for Joshua to cross the Jordan River.

Can God trust us to put away complaints and follow Him regardless of the conditions or climate of what we have been called to do? Can we control our feelings and rely on His grace to guide us to fulfillment? Are we willing to wait on God to complete His work in us? God will use those who honor leadership. Anyone can please leadership in the spotlight, but how will we react in the desert? Will we remain faithful in the dry times when it seems as though nothing we are doing is bearing any fruit?

In the vastness of problems and in the fallout of murmuring, is there steadfastness inside that the wilderness experience cannot shake, or rebellion will not budge, or jealously will not pollute? Can we be faithful under another person's ministry while waiting on God to bring our ministry into fruition? Can God bless the leadership and trust us not to sabotage the ministry? Will we be loyal, and not lazy, in service? Joshua's heart was never in question. He believed in Moses and followed him without reservation. We should walk so closely with our leader/mentor that all the questions that could arise in our hearts would never make it to the surface. God can be trusted. He is the keeper of our hearts. Do we have what it takes to remain faithful? Are we people of integrity?

God called a meeting with Joshua and informed him that Moses was dead. The stage was set. It was time for Joshua to come to the front-line to become not the armor-bearer but the bearer of arms. God was calling him. Joshua was now coming of age. It was time for him to fulfill his destiny. (By this, I don't mean he was chronologically old enough to be used of God, for physical age is not a concession in terms of God's will for our lives. Remember, David was but a lad when God first used him mightily.)

God was changing Joshua's position (remember, position is knowing who God is). Joshua was now going to know God for himself, not through the staff of Moses, but through the Jordan experience. If the Lord is going to use us, then it will be with the gifts He has given to us. We can admire another person's gifting, but we cannot cross the Jordan with copied material. Everything must be original. It is God's way or no way at all.

God was revealing Himself to Joshua, not only as the God of Moses but also as a real, personal God who could be trusted to lead and provide for His people. "For as I was with Moses, so will I be with thee...I will not fail thee nor forsake thee" (Joshua 1:5-9) assured the Lord to Joshua. God prepared Joshua through Moses. Now the Lord would detail him (bring him into maturity) and put the final touches on him. The Lord was personally going to guide and instruct Joshua because he had proven himself faithful and teachable. Resources always follow destiny. The lessons behind us will propel us to the crossing point, and we will need everything that God has taught us when we get there. This is the threshold of our destiny.

I believe the children of Israel had two problems. The first problem was following Moses *out of* Egypt. The second was in trusting and following Joshua *into* the Promised Land. However, I will discuss this issue later in the book.

A Necessary Action

The Jordan River experience is an example of what serves as a crucible in the life of every believer. You can liken it to the point of turning or crossing when our past visions meet our future realities. When you arrive at the bank of your Jordan River, you will have to know who God is in order to pass over to the other side and into your destiny. Remember this: In Egypt, you *were passed by*. At the Red Sea you *passed through*. But now, at the Jordan, it is time to *pass over*.

This turning point calls for action not reaction and decision not uncertainty. Going forward is the by-product of obedience, and obeying someone means believing they are worthy of our confidence. Navigating new crossing points takes faith. It involves the difference between what we know and whom we know!

Proverbially speaking, what we knew helped us to follow Moses out. Whom we know will take us over the Jordan. The crossing point is where we see the revealing of the promise and the fulfillment of the covenant. Before Moses died, the mantle of his anointing—the fire and passion of conviction and authority imparted unto him by God—was transferred to Joshua. Now, Joshua found himself in the transition of surrendering his will and accepting God's in its place. As a result, God was transforming him into the leader of the hour, molding him after His own perfect will. Joshua had been in the backdrop of Moses. It was time for him to take the place of leadership for which he had been groomed and mentored as the faithful armor-bearer of Moses.

Had he learned from Moses the vital lesson of devotion and reliance upon God? If there was any hidden agenda or ulterior motive in Joshua's heart and if he was not wholly devoted to the Lord God of Israel, it would surely surface here. It is one thing to call on God for yourself and another to call on Him on behalf of a nation. Leading yourself around and getting lost is bad enough, but getting lost with over a half million people looking to you for guidance is something altogether different!

As Joshua receives his marching orders from the Lord, it is imperative that he learns to follow His instructions precisely. The acknowledgment of God's abiding presence and His provision is given to Joshua, yet he is still faced with stiff opposition.

In Joshua 1:6, God commands Joshua to be "strong and very courageous." To be strong is to have a firm grip. To be very courageous is to have sound legs. In essence, God was telling Joshua to stand without letting go. We can also take this as encouragement in our day-to-day lives as well.

As we advance and as God's presence and provision are released to us step by step, we will face opposition as we follow the Father's will. As our relationship with the Father changes, so does our responsibility to Him. The lessons that God once allowed—the Red Sea experiences, our ignorance, our mountain experience—are lessons for which we will be held responsible as we mature. At our Jordan, we will be held accountable for what we have learned.

There have been times when we, too, had experiences like those Red-Sea-crossing moments, and the illumination of God came to us as it did to Moses during his mountain experience. But we have been found stooped in ignorance and in need of harsh lessons at times. Make no mistake about it; God might have allowed our lessons before, but, ultimately, we will be held responsible for learning from them.

When Joshua was accountable for himself, only he suffered if he failed to pray or seek God's face. Later, many lives could have been destroyed if he had failed to interpret correctly the will of the Lord for the corporate body. At the beginning of our personal relationship with the Lord, failure affected no one but us. However, as we grow and are in a position to affect more lives, we become responsible on a larger scale for a greater inheritance that was promised by God.

It is important to pay attention while we are in the Lord's

classroom, no matter the location of the class! It could be on a mountaintop or deep in a valley. Regardless, we need to learn whatever the Lord is trying to teach us if we are to succeed and to help others.

Do you have what it takes to cross over? Let's find out.

Have I not commanded thee? Be strong and of good courage; be not afraid, neither be thou dismayed: for the Lord thy God is with thee whithersoever thou goest. Then Joshua commanded the officers of the people, saying, pass through the host and command the people, saying prepare you victuals; for within three days ye shall pass over this Jordan, to go in to possess the land, which the Lord your God giveth you to possess it (Joshua 1:9-11).

There is a set time to cross over. God is very specific about timing. Naturally speaking, when fording a river, it has to be done at a certain time and place so that the water is shallow enough to cross. After the spring thaw, goods, people, and animals can be swept to destruction in the raging flood that thawing causes. Winter ice might look sturdy and safe, but at certain points it can break if it is crossed at the wrong time. So, you see, timing is everything!

God's agenda is absolutely flawless, and He knows the way we should take better than we do. God's timing is always preceded by his infallible Word. The Bible says, "When ye see the ark of the covenant of the Lord your God, and the priest bearing it, Get-up from your place and go after it" (Joshua 3:3). These words connote momentum: Get-up is followed by the action of go after it. In other words, when the Word of the Lords tells you to go, get moving!

49

The Secret of Success

There are three things we must do when following God:

- **Follow His direction**
- **Fulfill His will**
- **Faithfully follow His leading**

When Moses led the people, he did most of the work and bore most of the responsibility for the people. How closely he followed God determined the course of the entire assembly. Then it became Joshua's turn to stand in his place. It was his responsibility to follow God. It was up to the people to follow him as they had once followed Moses. In order to receive the victory, the people had to commit to obeying leadership. Moses had extended the rod, and God had moved in miracles, such as His parting of the Red Sea. However, a different dimension of relationship now existed. God was training his people to assume responsibility for being blessed.

God would not move on their behalf until they first did their part. They had to get up and go after His Word. Everything had been prepared, and the way had been made, yet it was the people's responsibility to take action. To benefit from this next dimension, we must get up and go! Here is the first key to success: *Go forward following God.*

X Marks the Spot

All things are now ready. Are you? This is where you stand declaring, "I'm not giving up any more ground. This means war!" What a statement it is to declare that you are ready to fight against all odds and yet trust the Lord! It is a test of faith when God asks, "Will you trust Me with your next move?" The word has been spoken, yet there is a problem that seems insurmountable in our eyes.

Because of the season that we are in, the river is flooded! What was once a trickle is now a raging torrent. We now ask the question, can God handle the floods of circumstances, hardship, financial loss, slander, persecution, sickness, and loss in our lives?

The answer is a resounding yes! When the enemy comes in like a flood, the Lord will lift up a standard against him. This miracle, however, will not happen by watching someone else do the work. We have to take a step of faith. X marks the spot! There is no time to retreat and no time to doubt, because the Lord is demanding that we advance.

Forward is where success is.
Forward is where deliverance is.
Forward is where your next level is.
Forward is where your breakthrough is.

Someone said that breakthroughs come when preparation meets opportunity. We need to go forward as Christian soldiers carrying the cross of Jesus! But, know this: The sword and spear will not win this battle. We cannot bargain with the river, and the river will not yield to our battle plans. It must be crossed, nonetheless! "Not by might, not by power, but by my spirit saith the Lord of host" (Zech. 4:6). X marked the spot where God proved to Joshua that He was with him. "This day will I begin to magnify thee in the sight of all Israel that they may know that as I was with Moses, so shall I be with thee" (Joshua 1:5). God has prepared a place of provision, but to get there, you will have to trust and follow the Lord.

51

Patience

Here is another key to success for you: *Waiting for the Lord to move is the only way to cross over into victory.* Go after it! Believe in the Lord. Hold onto His Word and receive His will. I can imagine that you are asking, "But how can I become fully persuaded that He will be there?" If God said it, believe it. Believe in His prophets and believe in His Word because it is unfailing. There will be times when the Lord will request that you do something that seems intimidating, but He will not let you be overwhelmed with what is going on around you; instead He would have you focus on His will.

That which the Lord promises, He is well able to perform. Joshua's passion for following orders was integrated into him from the years of obeying Moses. When Moses said to move, Joshua did so. When Moses asked him to spy out the new land, he readily did so. As a result, once again, God shows that He is true to His word. God's handiwork is faithfulness.

Joshua was in the right place at the right time and had the right heart to receive the promotion of God. Joshua was assured that since God had done miracles for Moses, He would surely do them for him, as well. The miracles you have seen God perform for others can be for you. Remember, faith comes by hearing, but results come by action. Trouble sometimes tries to mask deliverance with worry in an attempt to confuse us into thinking that the Lord is limited. But the good news is the Lord is not limited in any way, shape, or form in either His scope or His power.

Facts of Faith

God is not confined to explaining who He is. When He

does so, it is strictly out of His sovereign love for us. The crossing of the Jordan was not a parade to show off the omnipotence of God (His unlimited power). This event was the culmination and the triumph of a nation empowered to go forward. The Lord is showing us that we cannot count on anyone or anything other than Him. We must depend on Him to carry us through.

If you are one who thinks that everything that happens is predetermined and foreordained, you are only partly correct. Naturally, in this world you will find those who think only of themselves and their own interests. These people are completely indifferent to the needs, feelings, or desires of others. They are self-consumed. They trust in fate. They believe that they ultimately have no choice. This is one of the tools of deception that Satan uses to cloud our moment of deliverance. You need to know that falsehood is his game.

To some people, predetermination means "the choices in life are already made and the only alternative is to go along for the ride without comment or voice." The since-the-fight-is-fixed-nothing-else-matters attitude implies that the facts are unchangeable. If this were true, we would be most miserable because then we would be trapped in our present circumstances without hope of deliverance. However, believing in God requires us to have faith in spite of what the facts may be. What is deemed as the inevitable is often changed when God appears on the scene?

Filtering Is a Constant Process

Filtering means "allowing God to process the facts through His grace and divine will." Filtering enables us, through the

Holy Spirit, to eliminate the false elements of facts and cling to faithfulness. It involves giving God time to reveal His purpose for our lives. When the Lord is finished with us, there will not be any misunderstanding of His direction or His awesome presence. Filtering requires the surrendering of our will to His will and becoming transparent in thought, word, and deed. We were chosen to pass over. John 15:16 says,

Ye have not chosen me, but I have chosen you and ordained you that ye should go and bring forth fruit and that your fruit should remain that whatsoever ye shall ask of the Father in my name, He may give it you. These things I command you, that ye love one another. If the world hates you, ye know that it hated me before it hated you. If ye were of the world, the world would love his own: but because ye are not of the world, but I have chosen you out of the world, therefore the world hateth you.

I Peter 2:9 says,

But ye are a chosen generation a royal priesthood, an holy nation a peculiar people that ye should shew forth the praises of Him who called you out of darkness into his marvelous light.

The inheritance of being chosen carries with it the innate right to choose. When we accept the challenge to do God's will, we need to know that the adversary is determined to defeat us because we have been chosen. When the Lord chooses us, we become vessels of honor (Rom 9: 21-24). The selection process has nothing to do with ability but everything to do with availability. God will take us and mold us into something useful. "Not our will, but thine is done Lord Jesus" (Luke 22:42). When God chooses us and we acknowledge His Lordship, then He releases His purpose in our lives. A purpose is given when we are selected for service. Joshua 3:10 says, "And Joshua said, Hereby ye shall know that the living God is among you and that He will without fail drive out from before you the Canaanites, and the Hittites, and the Hivites." Everything that stands between us and the will of God will be moved.

Another secret of success is *to have the one and only living God among us*! Success will not become apparent just by having people with us. Having a large crowd of people will not guarantee victory, as Judge Gideon discovered. Gideon was told by God to gather some men together for a battle. Gideon collected about 32,000 men. God told Him that was too many. After the first cut, God said that there were still too many. So God excused all but 300 men and told Gideon that was enough for Him to work with. You see, God's provision is based upon His calling. When God calls and directs, provision follows.

When the provision is made, go after it! Don't try to settle for a better time or a better plan, just go after it. Don't wait for the flood to subside, go after it. Don't look for more people or more confirmations. When God says go, go on, knowing that He is in front and the path is already prepared. Just follow Him without question, for He is the only living God.

Beloved, the enemy will always have a "Hath God said..." prepared for you as He did with Eve in the garden. But when God speaks, you can depend on Him. So when God says to step into your Jordan River, get stepping! Step with the authority of His Word. I want to give you one last key to success in the acronym **S.T.E.P.**, which stands for Striving Toward Expected Provision. Receive the confirmation of His will. For when He could swear by none greater, He swore or confirmed it by Himself. Accept the supply of his provision. Go after it!

Challenge 5
JEHOVAH ROHI—
THE LORD MY SHEPHERD

Alerting—The Facts

Have a funeral service. All dead things must be buried. Light a candle! Say good-bye! It is time to settle it. The closure process was designed for healing. The Word says to lay aside every weight that brings unbalance. Yes, lay aside the weight. No, not shedding those extra pounds you carry, but putting away, cremating, burying, singing a hymn and going out leaving the remains of issues to be disposed of type weight. Not a memorial for an hour, but leaving it there forever. There is a memorial service we all need to have, every one of us, at varying levels of intensity and for any number of reasons.

Declaring—Your Role

Remember yesterday with fleeting fondness; learn from the pain; dead things are toxic and emit bacteria that we cannot live in. LET IT GO! If God intended for us to live in it, then He would bring it back. Think! If you store too much old stuff in your fridge or on your hard drive, it causes delays or decays. Be encouraged!

Activating—What Will You Do Now?

We hold onto stuff out of fear. We hold on because we are sometimes cowards. We hold on because it was better before than it looks right now. Some of us are holding onto people who are begging us to let them go. Some of us hold onto old hurts that should have been forgiven because it is safe. Nevertheless, it's a new day. Say this right now: "For all of the yesterdays I bury—Hallelujah!—I make room for the new tomorrows God will bring to me. Amen." Have a funeral and bury that thing. Sing that hymn. It is a challenge. Life is a challenge. We can meet it in God's strength.

Lord, do not bless what I am doing, help me to do what You are blessing!

Chapter 6

Lead Me, Guide Me

As we have seen, the two problems the children of Egypt had were following Moses out of Egypt (leaving) and following Joshua into the Promised Land (entering).

Leaving encompasses the surrendering of all things past, and it is the resolve of past lives, issues, attitudes, agendas, and methods of operations. Utilizing the knowledge of when to leave is powerful. Leaving and entering can leave you feeling vulnerable and exposed. Leaving requires that the comfort zone be left behind. *Entering* can be defined as "the coming into divine order and acceptance of God's will for your life."

In the fall of 1997, I was in a struggle between my will and God's purpose. Although I was willing to go after it, I wanted better terms. Sitting in my office one night, while I was toiling in the middle of my yes-I'll-do-it-but-wait-a-minute-posture, the Lord gave me a vision. In the vision, I was standing by the seashore along with my wife, Marion. To the right of me was a large framed boat floating in the water. To the left of me was an enormous group of familiar people. While I could not distinguish any one face, I felt very comfortable with them. It was like being in front of a fireplace on a cold winter night while drinking hot chocolate.

In an instant, our direction and position was changed. Marion and I were now in the boat, sailing away from the group of people. As we sailed, the people became smaller and smaller until they completely vanished into a mist that appeared out of nowhere. It was very disheartening and uncomfortable because I had lost sight of the familiar. I later discovered that the Lord was moving me from comfort to destiny.

Leaving one stage of life and entering another stage requires faith. No level of teaching can prepare you for the move of God. You will never have enough training, education or strength to equip you for your destiny. Leaving and entering has much to do with trusting that God knows what's best for you. The Spirit of God will probe you to check your readiness to obey. This is not just a geographical move, but a mind-set move. You have heard the phrase "You can lead a horse to water but can't make him drink." Entrapment starts in the mind with doubt and fear as its yoke-fellows. The struggle in breaking free is learning that leaving begins in your spirit before it happens in your body. "For as a man thinks, so is he" (Prov. 23:7).

I believe that the reason we have so much trouble with leaving the past behind is that people do not want closure. Instead they crave enclosure. That's the trap! The enemy wants to enclose you in your past to prevent you from pursuing your future. The fear of following God is a deception of the devil. It is a desperate plot to dissuade you from the purpose and promise of God, the One who chose you.

Cover-Up vs. Closing Up

The first cover-up happened in the Garden of Eden when Satan persuaded Adam and Eve that leaving the Word of God would help them enter the perfect will of God.

The end result was that they had to cover up what they had messed up. They had failed to close off the voice of Satan from their spirits and, as a result, lost it all. What did they lose? I call it the five P's:

Purpose
Power
Protection
Provision
Peace

Yes, it was all lost because they did not enclose their areas of exposure. In this case, it was the knowledge of good and evil in their lives. Instead of trusting God, when He alone knew what was best for them, they entrusted their lives to someone who had not invested anything in them, someone who had no personal connection to them and did not care at all about them. Satan used them, trying to get back at God for kicking him out of heaven.

His sole purpose was to destroy their relationship with the Father God. Because they did not close themselves off from Satan, they were forced to cover up from God. The same is true in your life; if you don't close yourselves off from and deal with the weakness in your life, then you, too, will try to cover up your sins with fig leaves. You must understand that covering-up consumes time and causes separation from your heavenly Father. You cannot cover up your past. You must move on with life and close the door to your past forever so that you can enter into your destiny.

Entering In

Remember the word which Moses the servant of the Lord commanded you saying the Lord your God hath given you rest and this land (Joshua 1:13).

Entering in is coming into divine order. Entering into the Lord's rest will bring peace. Entering means "receiving what the Lord has spoken." No military strategies are set in place, and no method of approach is called for. When God moves, there are no boundaries that cannot be overcome. No gulf is too great, no river too wide, and no mountain too high. Lodged in His protective arms is the divine providence of God who sees in advance what we need and makes provision for it. Remember this, He will never violate our will in order to bless us. Jesus said that He could not do many miracles in His hometown because they would not believe in Him. To be blessed is to submit to God's way, to believe in His Word, and to rely on His plan for your life. Enter in; there is safety and security in His redemptive and protective arms.

What is our purpose as far as God is concerned? How does He view us? The Lord is not in the personality business. He sees our hearts and souls, not our carnal bodies, as man does. Our God is in the relationship business. The Lord is concerned with where we are as it relates to spirituality and community. He will meet us at our point of need. His benefits are based on His resources, not ours. Our God is the initiator of faith. Moses endured (stood firm) because he saw the invisible.

> Hebrews 11:27 says, *"By faith He forsook Egypt, not fearing the wrath of the king: for He endured, as seeing him who is invisible."*

So, Moses endured because he saw Him who is invisible. We readily understand and accept things that are seen, but the things we cannot see are what cause us the greatest conflict within our spirit. The Lord is the initiator of faith, but acceptance of this fact can be clouded by unbelief.

How can you count on someone whom you cannot see who is telling you to do something you have never done? Trying to fathom God will drive you crazy. Don't try to do it! Relax and let Him lead you. He is beyond finding out, figuring out, or faking out. The Lord does not bluff. He is not looking for answers to our situation. He is the answer!

The King, The Den, The Lions

> *Then this Daniel was preferred above the presidents and the princes, because an excellent spirit was in him: and the king thought to set him over the whole realm. Then the presidents and princes sought to find occasion against Daniel concerning the kingdom; but they could find none occasion nor fault; forasmuch as He was faithful, neither was there any error or fault found in him* (Daniel 6:3-4).

Have you ever told the Lord to have His way in your life, and He responded with a trial? I have! I found out that where there is no cross, there will be no crown, and for my faith to be valid, it must be put to the test. King Darius, who was tricked into placing Daniel inside a den of lions because Daniel believed in his invisible God. The facts are these:

1) King Darius was deceived into jailing Daniel in the lion's den because of jealousy. Daniel prayed three times a day to God. He was fervent and consistent. He exuded a pattern of faithfulness.

2) The den was a furnace of reality. However, Daniel was delivered before he was placed in the dilemma. (God has a way out even before we get into the furnace.) The den caused Daniel and the King to see the authority and provision of God.

3) The lions were visible, audible, and hungry. The enemy is present; however, he is limited in his ability to harm us.

4) Daniel's faith was on trial. There is no court of appeals to suspend the trying of our faith, but a trial has limits on its authority to perform certain destructive acts because our Father is in control at all times.

While trials place our faith under examination, God is faithful to make a way of escape for us right under the nose of the enemy. What Daniel needed, could not be seen or heard. He needed a miracle. Your faith will be tempered in the furnace of reality. What is your furnace of reality? It is, indeed, your visible problems. And they are about to be out-flanked by an invisible God who is all-powerful, who has dominion over all, and to whom all majesty belongs. Daniel believed God even when the cards were stacked against him. The validity of his faith was tried, and he was victorious because he stood strong. Is seeing believing? Lets look at some facts. Seeing equates to sight. Believing equates to faith; therefore, vision is not faith, for if you can see a thing, why hope for it?

Sight is perception	**Faith is reception**
Sight is tangible	**Faith is intangible**
Sight is concrete	**Faith is abstract**

Sight is not believing. Believing and trusting God is seeing! When you trust God through faith, you will see the victory. If you believe in the Lord, then you will experience His peace. Every test has its time. Ecclesiastes 3:1 says, "To everything there is a season and a time to every purpose under the heavens." God has set a beginning and an ending to everything in your life. Nothing will last forever except His Word. God says, "Heaven and earth shall pass away but my word will never pass away" (Matt. 24:35).

...But God is faithful, who will not suffer you to be tempted above that ye are able, but will with the temptation also make a way to escape that ye may be able to bear it (1 Cor. 10:13).

He Will Share It, So You Can Bear It

The Lord's invested interest in us constrains Him to help

us. He will make a way to escape! When I see the word escape, I know that the literal meaning is "to get out of something." My question is, does escape actually mean "freedom for the escapee"? It does when God is in the picture. As far as the world's system is concerned, it does not. Escape in the world's system is an illusion, a smoke screen of deception. In the world's system, escape is a getaway, a temporary relief. More commonly called R and R (rest and relaxation).

Escaping is not something accomplished through physical means. Nothing man-made will give permanence to one's deliverance. Man's failed ability to cope with stress is shown throughout history. History reveals that humans are fragile creatures. We have created exotic getaways such as resorts with white sand beaches, palm trees, and crystal blue waters. These exotic islands were developed for people who want to escape stress or the humdrum of life. Some people choose to escape through their jobs and careers. Others use the television or video arcades to escape the furnace of reality. There are others who use drugs, sex, alcohol, or gambling as an escape. Some people even use the church to help them to escape. The only true escape from the reality of the furnace is to have a relationship with God. The Lord will make a way of escape, and you will be delivered. In Him you will find permanent rest.

Seasons

Seasons represent levels of growth through testing. While provision is the spiritual thermostat that helps us adjust to the atmosphere (level of the furnace), time teaches us that God is faithful and will not allow us to be destroyed. Seasons are the Lord's testing ground. Time gives us an opportunity to respond to His divine will. Seasons determine specific moments in the span of time, but they have no bearing on the promise of God in times of controversy. "When the enemy comes in like a flood the Lord will lift up a standard against him" (Isa. 59:19). During God's seasons, there are periods of favor. Favor is always preceded by testing.

Shadrach, Meshach, Abed-nego

If it be so our God whom we serve is able to deliver us from the burning fiery furnace, and He will deliver us out of thine hand, O King! (Daniel 3:17).

It may seem strange that the Christian lifestyle is forged out of the battleground and not a playground. We are in a battle, and we are fighting for our lives. The information that the enemy does not want us to know is there is triumph before the trial and blessing before the battle.

When we are in a test, the method of deliverance is not important, but the assurance of the deliverance is. In other words, it does not matter how God delivers, as long as we know He will deliver.

To win the battle there are three important things we must do or have:

1) **Know who the enemy is—**
The Bible says that we are not ignorant of his devices (Corinthians 2:11).

2) **Possess power—**
That is the Holy Spirit dwelling on the inside.

3) **Have protection—**
Put on the whole armor of God.

Once we resolve to obey God completely, it is easy to assume that life will go more smoothly. When things go smoothly, we tend to believe that this proves that we are in God's will. However, nothing could be further from the truth! If that were true, then every time we ran into obstacles, we would be out of God's will. Do you see what a roller coaster ride that would be? Things can go haywire while we are right in the middle of the will of God.

Although Shadrach, Meshach and Abed-nego honored God with excellence, their season of testing arrived. The enemy will try to analyze, discourage, and anticipate the next move of God in our lives. But whatever he tries, we need to remain steadfast. Although they actually feared the furnace, it did not stop them from trusting whom they loved. God says that when we trust Him, no weapon formed against us shall prosper. The test is coming, so don't faint. Hold on!

These three Hebrews trusted God for better and for worse. They were thrown into a fiery furnace for their trouble, yet they did not faint. They came out of that furnace smelling like a rose because God was with them.

How to overcome during a time of testing:
1) Learn to trust God in your furnace; He is your exit.

2)   Don't let circumstances control your decisions.

3)   Never take God for granted. He is Lord. Commit to Him.

4)   Don't give the enemy a foothold, or he will create a stronghold!

5)   Call on the name of Jesus. He will not forsake you.

In the book of James it says, "Blessed is the man that endureth temptation for when he is tried he shall receive the crown of life which the Lord hath promised to them that love him" (James 1:12).

Challenge 6
JEHOVAH JIREH—
THE LORD MY PROVIDER

Alerting—The Facts

From time to time, we all go back to the stuff I call trash. Clean it out! We remember compliments for a moment but insults for 20 years. We have become garbage collectors. Some situations have confronted us and left us a little unsettled. We must trust God, and allow Him to let us graduate from class LET-IT-GO 101. It's a hard thing to let go of the past. However, I did some of that today. I emptied my personal trashcan of some things I had been holding onto for years. What do I mean? I released from my spirit-man everything that was keeping me from becoming whole and stunting my growth. I cannot describe the weightlessness I felt as I laid aside the weight. I had carried around resentment and pain. I had a bag of hurt feelings. Oh, they were justified in my eyes, all right. I had a right to be hurt and angry. However, I didn't have a right not to forgive, because I was trying to please God. I was continually asking Him to create in me a clean heart and renew a right spirit within me every day, except for one little thing—I had this can of trash. God wants to fill our spirits with love, joy and peace. He wants to renew and restore, but we have no place for what He has for us because our cans are full of old dead stuff. LET-IT-GO!

Declaring—Your Role

We must take out the trash of dead things in our lives that will hold us back. Sometimes our trashcan is so full, but we don't realize it. Think about this for a minute. If a bank called and told you to bring a container to them so that they could fill it to the brim with money, would you take a full piece of luggage or a purse that was running over? No! You would clean out the largest thing you had and rush to the bank and say, "fill 'er up." Some of us are professional students enrolled at the University of Unforgiveness and Resentment. It's toxic! If we're not careful, resentments can build, and we will close ourselves off from God's blessing.

Activating—What Will You Do Now?

We often talk about being brokenhearted. We all have been. The Lord allowed me to take some pieces out of my trash can and get rid of them to make more room for Him in my heart. Repeat this prayer of surrender:

Lord, help me release the past and its hurts so that I can move forward to my destiny. Help me to surrender some major "stuff" and major people, not to give up on them, or quit believing in them, but, God, release me from handling them mentally and emotionally anymore. So, Lord, I surrender all things that have been keeping me tied up mentally and emotionally. Amen.

Quit holding onto the pain or hurt, whatever it is. Pray, look up, and clean out your trashcan. Be free.

Chapter 7

You Can't Turn Back Now; God Is Here!

The word "now" is an adverb, an action word. It means "move quickly or immediately." While looking at the word now, I came up with the acronym N.O.W.—No Other Way. When we are in trouble, there is no way out except through Jesus Christ. However, when we reverse the word, it spells WON! We cannot quit and turn back because we have already WON.

Risk is always present in this life. It is risky to ride a bike or drive a car. It is risky to take a 30-minute commercial flight. Risk involves a certain amount of trust. It takes faith to risk anything in life. Faith in God is worth any risk. Hebrews 11:34 says,

*By faith the faithful quenched the violence of fire and es-
caped the edge of the sword out of weakness were made
strong, waxed valiant in fight turned to flight the armies of
the alien.*

Whatever the situation may be, God's way is the only safe
way out of it. Faith in God is the foundation of Christianity,
and it has three characteristics: faith is *microscopic*—it sees
what is invisible to the naked eye; faith is *telescopic*—it sees
farther than the scope of our natural vision; faith is
periscopic—it sees above the circumstances of life.

The boundaries of our faith are restricted only by us. Faith
is the response we give to God after receiving His Word. We
need to forget what we know and trust Him. God transcends
our logic and understanding. To know God is to trust Him.
Faith draws the line between what we will and will not accept
in life.

Confidence is triumph dressed incognito. The ability to
see through obstacles is a key to our victory. This takes the
anointing of the Lord. He will not anoint where He does not
plan to deliver. To dwell with God means to walk with Him to
the end.

How do we maintain confidence in the midst of trouble?
We must ask God. Guidance and protection are the trademarks of our Lord. We will never be without His help or out of
the realm of His protection. "In all thy ways acknowledge him,
He will direct your path" (Prov. 3:6). The Lord is our helper,
guide, and leader. He is our strong tower (protection) and our
fortress. He is the only true example of a living, reigning
fortress. Our God reigns! Hallelujah!

The Lord is mobile. He moves and He moves. I heard one
preacher say, "God only steers moving vehicles." He is a God

of action and never does anything without a purpose. Genesis 1 says, "And the earth was without form and void: and darkness was upon the face of the deep. And the Spirit of God moved upon the face of the waters" (Gen. 1:2-3). He is moving for us and ahead of us. The children of Israel knew God as their guide and protector. He led them while they were in the wilderness and through many trials.

Since the beginning of creation, Satan's desire has been to impose his will upon mankind. He has done so by using conflict as one of his many weapons. Military action has been defined in terms of the ability of an adversary to achieve supremacy over an enemy in three fields of action: mobility, firepower, and security.

Our enemy will first try to immobilize us through depression, doubt, and hopelessness. He also likes to use his ace-in-the-hole—fear—to render many of us paralyzed. The word paralyzed naturally gives a strong impression of one being left crippled after a trauma of some sort.

The word "fear" gives the impression that life and conflict become so difficult and strenuous that a person is reduced in strength so that it is difficult for him to stand against an opposing force. Fear can be so hard to deal with that even considering mustering the strength to defeat it can render us mentally and physically immobile.

Firepower

The enemy will try to defeat us through our own lack of firepower. Satan's firepower is effective, but his arsenal is limited; he uses darts of fire. His objective is to steal, kill, and to destroy (John 10:10). He causes major damage and discouragement through pain. He often disfigures us with hurt and disrupts us with confusion. He will fire flaming arrows of conflict to thwart our emotional stamina. His intent is to spiritually kill us.

> *Be self-controlled and alert. Your enemy the devil prowls around like a roaring lion looking for someone to devour* (1 Peter 5:8 TLB).

The Lord also says, *"Behold I give unto you power to tread on serpents and scorpions and over all the power of the enemy: and nothing shall by any means hurt you"* (Luke 10:19).

The enemy wants to do three things:

1) Probe us for vital information and pertinent facts that will lead him to any weak or unprotected areas in our lives. With this, he can have maximum effect when attacking us (remember Job).

2) Target us so that he does not miss his mark. With us as a target, his focus is more direct and specific when he sets the attack. He wants to hit only what is vital.

3) Shoot us by firing at us at every available moment. He wants to do anything that will cause hurt, harm, or death. However, the Holy Spirit is our arsenal, and He is fully capable of handling any attack of any magnitude from the enemy. One of his many attributes is firepower.

Act 1:8 says, "After the Holy Ghost shall come upon you,

ye shall have (dynamos) or dynamite power." The explosive power of the Holy Spirit is more than a match for the enemy. No weapon formed against us shall prosper! This clearly means that it shall not have the ability to hurt us. The enemy tries to invade our security, which is our peace. The Lord, however, has promised that if we keep our minds on Him, then He will keep us in perfect peace. Make this declaration with me now: "Peace is not an option for me but a benefit. No matter how long or hard the battle, keeping my mind stayed on Jesus will keep me in perfect peace."

The object is not to see through one another but to see one another through.—Peter Devries

Closed Caption Viewing

How does God speak to us? God will reveal His way through His Word. God gets our attention by helping us realize our inability to handle conflict without him. The Lord says, "For without me ye can do nothing" (John 15:5). God shows Himself to us in many different ways and for many purposes. God will never reveal Himself with the sheer intention of demonstrating that He is superior in thought, word, or deed. That is not the purpose of revelation for us.

His expressions deal with our ego so that we don't think more highly of ourselves than we ought to. Sometimes the Lord will take us to places where He can discuss His purposes with us. Perhaps He will join us in the fire as He did with the three Hebrew men. He may come into the water as He did for Joshua at the Jordan River, or He may come in a whirlwind in the manner by which He showed Himself to Ezekiel. He may even speak in a still small voice as He did for the prophet Elijah. Nevertheless, the Lord will choose the time and place for your close encounter with Him.

Who would not want to respond to a God who so lovingly beckons us? When He calls, we must answer Him. Comfort comes with covenant; covenant offers covering; covering gives protection. God calls us because there is a void in the kingdom. There is a conflict that rages within us as we try to decide the difference between will and wisdom, our public personas versus our private ones. Behind closed doors, we often find ourselves dealing with who we really are in contrast to who we would like to be.

Struggles Are Good

Please don't misunderstand me. I am not a proponent of struggle, for the contrary is true, but I do believe we can learn something from the struggle itself. As strange as it may sound, struggles prepare us for freedom. As believers we must view struggles as positive because they have a way of showing us that there is advancement on the horizon!

While in the height of struggling, often we become more settled in our faith. The foundation of our faith in God becomes more sure than it was prior to the struggle.

As the baby chick grows in its contemporary environment, everything it needs is provided for it inside its shell. The elements of covering, protection, and nourishment are readily seen. As the chick matures and comes closer to hatching, what is not so apparent (because of the covering of the shell) is the fact the chick is struggling while it is covered and protected. Conflict is present in the shell. As it grows, what once provided ample room has now become tight and uncomfortable. The struggle is not meant for punishment. It is not to create public reaction or speculation. In fact, the process of the breakthrough saves the chick from certain death. But if the mother has to help it out, it will be weak and dependent for all of its life. The struggle is a matter of life or death. If the chick does not emerge in time, its covering will become a tomb; therefore, its exodus is the only way to survive. Struggles in life are worth the effort we put forth to ensure that we make it out of them.

So, don't find yourself despising struggles for the added tension they bring, but see them as another test that requires additional effort to pass. Remember, struggles are temporary, and you should not allow yourself to be consumed by them. This too shall pass! Turn your struggles into a strategy for action. If you follow God's strategies, they will give you options. Therefore, plan for peace, and you will turn your struggle into a strategy for peace. Struggles are indicators that deliverance is near. The struggles of life can cause us to focus on our immediate needs, but the Lord wants us to utilize the Holy Spirit to direct us into all truth.

Remember, the circumstances of deliverance are not important; the assurance of the deliverance is. The circumstances can be critical, but they are not the conclusion. The Lord will have something to say before it's all over.

Comprehension is what you have recognized as a fact, but perception is what your mind's eye has beheld, which has nothing to do with what the final outcome will be. God's assurance gives steadfastness, or what I like to call stick-to-it-iveness. When unjustified criticism comes, sometimes failure seems most likely. Don't give up! Struggle is OK. Strain for your future. Fight for it. It is not in our nature to quit without a fight. Press on. Deliverance comes through faithfulness.

When a pregnant woman is about to deliver a child, she gets uncomfortable and irritable. Her body has changed to get ready to give birth. However, as the time to deliver approaches, pain is present. There is never birth without pain. Anything worth conceiving is worth struggling for. Jacob actually waited at Bethel to cross Jordan to meet his intense competition, Esau, better known as his struggle. Earlier that day, he sent everyone else ahead. But that night, Jacob did meet with intensity. He found himself grabbing hold of a man and wrestling with him until the breaking of day! The man adjured Jacob to release him, but Jacob somehow felt within himself that there was a blessing in the struggle. So he answered, "I will not let you go until you bless me!" (Gen. 32:26) What could Jacob have meant? What was he thinking of? In other words, Jacob said, "I will not release you from this struggle until you make a deposit into my life." It turns out that the "man" was an angel of the most high God. You see, Jacob knew, as you should know, that when God makes a deposit in your life, it increases your worth.

The Stress Test

Can you pass a stress test? God will inevitability place us in positions where we will be tested. For instance, if you go to the doctor's office for an examination and, during the course of the exam, irregular patterns are found in your heart, the only way to make a proper diagnosis is to subject your body to further testing. The stress test is one such test. It includes running on a treadmill for several minutes to increase the load on the heart by raising its rate. With this, the blood flowing through the circulatory system will increase throughout the body.

The entire respiratory system, which includes the lungs, will also increase significantly. It is through this process that the doctor gauges the heart's and body's abilities to function under duress—the power used to overcome resistance or stress, a weight placed on something or someone important. When the body performs well under the load of the stress test, the doctor declares that the body is performing as it should.

However, when it does not perform well, the doctor looks for ways to prevent a disaster from occurring. God will sometimes place us in areas and positions that will put us under stress. But God is not trying to sabotage His servants. God wants to reveal through the test the areas we need to give attention to. The amazing thing about the stress test is that its purpose is not only to show the patient where their physical vulnerabilities are but also to reveal where the strengths are. So when God tests us, He is not simply giving us a list of fixer-uppers. He is providing us with the precise fact that our strength is made perfect in weakness. It is only when we understand our weakness that He will make us strong. God will subsidize our strength and provide us with tools to enable us to rise above the stress of life.

Americans are constantly bombarded with perplexities that cause stress. Most of us are so stressed out that something as common as getting to work and back home again without collapsing is nothing short of a miracle. The levels of stress that people are subjected to are phenomenal: at home, in our finances, and in our ministry. Stress is in our general living.

The stress levels in daily life are so intense that people are literally "stressing for success," and what follows, no less, are ulcers and heart attacks, which have become common place in our society. There is an old saying, "If you can't stand the heat get out of the kitchen," but I say that it was never God's intention for us to be stressed out by life. He came that we might have life, and that, more abundantly!

The Lord may stretch us out through the process of growth and maturity, but He'll never stress us out. God's tests reveal character and never conceal character. He will bless but never burden us. His desire is to fortify us for our future. God loves and cares for His people. His love is shown in the shed blood of His Son Jesus Christ. He was in all points tempted as we are, yet He was without sin. The Bible says, "We have not a high priest that is unmindful of the things we go through" (Heb.. 4:15). Nothing shall separate us from His love! So you can't turn back now! You have already won!

Challenge 7
JEHOVAH ELYON—
THE LORD MOST HIGH

Alerting—The Facts

There's a time for all things. We take His plan so lightly. We buy planners. We check the dates. We check the weather. We celebrate birthdays. We quote "To everything there is a time and season" (Ecc. 3:1), yet forget that the master time-giver and time-keeper is God. We fail to check with Him daily and seek the task that He has for us to do that day. In business, we tell one another to go with the flow. Whose flow? He is the master planner and our intimate Father, our hands-on designer and creator. We talk about being yielded vessels, then when a situation comes up that requires us to yield, we seem to forget what it means to be flexible and pliable and committed to the point where we lose our own flesh and lay trusting in His Spirit. We lose ourselves in things and in earthen vessels that give no return, and cry because there is no fulfillment.

Declaring—Your Role

God says, "It's time to turn it around." The natural man does not comprehend spiritual things, but God uses the natural to teach us spiritual principles. Sunup and sundown, we often take years for granted that we can't get back. *Carpe diem* means "Seize the day." However, you cannot seize a day God does not give to you. Ask daily for God to put you to work and use His time to get to know Him better, seizing the time.

Activating—What Will You Do Now?

Obedience is truly better than sacrifice. Truly, while all things do work together for good, it is heartbreaking to devote yourself to futile works. This is not a game, God is not Captain Hook, and none of us are meant to be Peter Pan. He has given us a world, and one of the most precious gifts in it, besides salvation, is time. Take a few minutes each day and journal where your time was spent. Then, ask yourself, was God pleased in all of it? Tell the Lord, "Lord, don't bless what I'm doing, but help me to do what you are blessing.

Breakthrough comes when opportunity meets preparation.

Chapter 8

Whom Do You Resemble?

The important thing is this: be ready at any moment to sacrifice what we are for what we could become.
—Charles Dubois

When Jesus came into the coast of Caesarea Philippi, He asked his disciples saying. Whom do men say that I the Son of man am? And they said, some say that thou art John the Baptist: some, Elias: and others, Jeremias, of one of the prophets. He saith unto them. But whom say ye that I am? And Simon Peter answered and said; Thou art the Christ, the Son of the living God. And Jesus answered and said unto him. Blessed art thou, Simon Bar-Jonas: for flesh and blood hath not revealed it unto thee, but my father which is in Heaven (Matt. 16:13-17).

Whom Do You Resemble?

Have you ever noticed that people are a curious lot? For example, a nursery filled with babies becomes a layout for the curious to study. They stand looking and wondering which baby belongs to which parent while they point out obvious similarities and pointed differences. People will always want to categorize who and what we are, based on what they merely see. However, the hidden realities in life usually rise to the surface and become noticeable at times of crisis or exposure.

Progress does not come without sacrifice. Jesus asked, "Who do men say that I am?" Jesus did not ask the question merely to receive information. He was preparing the disciples to live a life without His physical presence. He wanted them to be sure of who He was. In order to understand what His purpose was, they needed to know who He was. But how were the disciples to react to the truth of His identity?

The reality of the disciple's answers gave weight to the conclusion that they were not sure if He was the Christ. He had shown them trace elements of power, and there were noticeable similarities between His life and what was prophesied in the Scriptures. However, the disciples had not yet understood His motives for ministry. Was He a determined revolutionist or a powerful revelation? There was a hidden quality in Jesus that propelled Him to His destiny.

Exposure reveals identity. One of Jesus' key objectives was to become transparent to His disciples. Jesus will only reveal Himself to those who are in covenant (agreement and commitment) with Him. How you view God will determine your relationship with Him. If He has not been revealed to you, you will never have an understanding of who He is.

While He yet spake, behold, a bright cloud overshadowed them: and behold a voice out of the cloud, which said this is my beloved Son, in whom I am well pleased: Hear ye him (Matt. 17:5).

It was not until the heavenly Father knew the disciples' hearts that He revealed his heart to them. "This is my beloved Son in whom I am well pleased." The Father specified this time to unveil and validate the identity of His son. Son-light always exposes. The gospel of John says, "In him was the life and the life was the light of men. The light shines in darkness and the darkness comprehended it not" (John 1:5).

The Stirring of Issues

Crisis has a way of bringing hidden things to the surface. When I was a small boy, I used to frequently go fishing. One day at Pine Lake, in Youngstown, Ohio, I was standing on the bank fishing, and as I looked through the water, I noticed that there were baby fish trying to capture my bait.

After watching for a while, I decided to see if I could catch them and use them as bait to land a bigger fish. So I rolled up my pants legs, and stepped slowly into the clear water with net in hand. As I moved towards the fish, something strange happened. The water started to become muddy. With every step I took, the clear water became cloudier, until I could not see anything at all. There was no alternative fishing method at this point. I was forced to leave the lake because my vision was severely impaired. The stirring of the mud had thwarted my attempt to catch the fish. They were still in the lake, but I could not see them. As for the mud, it was there all the time, yet I could not see it because it was settled in its position on the bed of the lake. It was not until I stepped in and disturbed it that it became noticeable. In this life, we go toward our desired end only to step into issues that stir up crises.

As it was in that lake, crisis will arise to cloud your vision and discourage your purpose. However, don't panic, because God is still in control. Crisis can cause you to retreat, but stand still until His will is clear. As I stated earlier, seeing is not believing, believing is seeing. We walk by faith not by sight.

Hidden Qualities

And when He was demanded of the Pharisees when the kingdom of God should come, He answered them and said, "the kingdom of God cometh not with observation: [vision] neither shall they say, lo her. [location], or there, [direction] for behold the kingdom of God is within you" (Luke 17:20-21).

"But whom say ye that I am?" is Jesus' question. The answer is, He is our revelation. Whom do we resemble? We should resemble our heavenly Father; His traits should be evident in our lives. After all, we were created in His image and likeness. Jesus is aware of everything that we are and will ever be. There are hidden qualities inside of us. We just need to stir them up. By allowing our hidden qualities to surface, we remove ourselves from self-doubt and just do the thing that is in us. 2 Tim 1:6 says,

Wherefore I put thee in remembrance that thou stir up the gift of God, which is in thee by the putting on of my hands.

The Lord will show us His will as we faithfully walk with Him more and more each day. To become more like Him, we must spend time with Him. To whom is the arm of the Lord revealed? To those who are persuaded that He is the Christ, the Son of the living God. It is apparent whose child we are.

The Lord continues to reveal Himself through His Word. God is propelling us towards our destiny. We have within us hidden qualities that the Lord can use. We must not allow crisis or the issues of life to cloud our vision of who we are.

Challenge 8
JEHOVAH SHALOM—
THE LORD OUR PEACE

Alerting—The Facts

Many times we labor before the Lord about things, sighing and weeping sometimes, because it appears or seems that He has not answered our request. We sometimes disobey God by being anxious, when He so clearly says to us to be anxious for nothing and to cast our cares on Him because He cares for us. He reminds us, yet we ask every time we talk to Him when He is going to take care of this or that. Leave it to God. I don't know how many of you remember that cute little toy called the Jack-in-the-Box. After you wind the little handle, at some point, a little clown-looking figure jumps up. It thrills some kids, but others are afraid of it. I don't know about you, but no matter how many times that little clown pops out, I jump.

If you're waiting on God and He is not responding fast enough, you want to be let go. You're all wound up like a Jack-in-the-Box. Ask God for patience because He knows when it's time for you to come out of the box.

Declaring—Your Role

If we wait on Him and don't touch that tiny little metal crank, we will be better off. You don't have to worry about what will jump out at you if you wait on an almighty, omnipotent, and omniscient God.

Activating—What Will You Do Now?

Remember the scripture, "Wait on the Lord and be of good courage" (Psalm 27:14). There's the answer. You don't have to jump. You don't have to fear that some menacing little clown-figure will pop up in your life. God knows our absolute perfect best. He may be preparing a better answer than we could have ever imagined. Wait on the Lord. "Wait," I say, "on the Lord." Then when that Jack comes out, you won't jump. His ways are perfect, and He perfects all that concerns you. Trust Him.

Success is a journey not a destination.

Chapter 9

Hold Your Fire!

And I said I will not speak any more in his name, but I could not control myself, His word is like a fire swelling up in my spirit. I couldn't hold it (Jer. 20:9 TLB).

Discouragement can cripple you beyond belief; it can grip you like a wild animal that has found its prey and goes in for the kill. However, experience has taught me not to cash in my chips too quickly. We cannot always run away, but instead we must stand our ground in spite of life and its circumstances. If we do not quit, eventually things will change for the better. Caution can cause you to pause when you should forge ahead. Being overly cautious when trusting God actually means that fear is present. Inside of you is the God given ability to persevere in the midst of dire circumstances, so don't quit before you reach your goal.

When there is conflict in our spirit, it will cause us to alter our direction and take the wrong course of action. Whether we are advancing or resolving, we must remain confident in God. In the heat of battle, those who hold their fire will win. The epic Civil War battles that I watched on TV as a boy showed me that when forces approached the enemy by marching toward them, the enemy soldiers would barricade themselves behind trees and wagons. The command was given that no one was to shoot until they could see the whites of their eyes. At the point of white-eye visibility, the enemy is as close as possible so that every shot will count. This kind of military conquest means that one force has defeated the other in battle and the victor gets the spoils.

Don't relinquish yet! Do not throw in the towel. Many victories have happened in the last minute or last seconds. Stand strong! Declare right now, "This is where I stand, and I am not giving up any more ground!"

Jeremiah was called the weeping prophet because he constantly interceded for Israel. As he prayed, he hoped that Israel would repent of their rebellion and turn back to God. However, there was no success. The more he prayed and cried out to God, the worse they became. During this time, Jeremiah was not on the Top-Ten-Most-Influential-People-in-the-Kingdom list. Jeremiah preached in a day when people generally were not seeking God as people do today. Let me put it this way, if Jeremiah had held a Bible conference at that time, it would have lacked conferees! It is certain that his memoirs were not on the bestseller list, either!

After preaching a poignant message with great passion for 40 years in the southern kingdom of Judah, he had no claim to fame, and no one would even listen to him. Jeremiah was alone and isolated. His message was not popular, and to make matters worse (if that was possible), he was imprisoned for it. Imagine what it must have been like to have a word from the Lord that upset the very fiber of the kingdom. Jeremiah was placed in a pit and left to die for preaching the word that he believed so strongly. How forsaken he must have felt. I can just see his heart dripping its essence like water from a cracked pipe. Jeremiah was in dire straits in that pit of persecution. He wanted to rescind his calling and mark it, "return to sender, address unknown." Many people doubt their ministry and question whether God will ever use them.

These emotions can put you on a downward spiral into despair and strip you of your courage and weaken your strength. In his pit, Jeremiah stood alone and felt rejected. His heart cried out, "Why?" In turn he made a premature confession based on his present condition. He said that he would not preach anymore in His name. At this point, I can just see Jeremiah's head on a slow descent and his chin resting on his own chest. If it happened to him, surely it can happen to you. But I say to you as you read this book, lift up your head! The Lord will make a way because He is Jehovah Jireh, God, our provider. Psalm 34:19 says, "Many are the afflictions of the righteous: but the Lord delivereth him out of them all." Isaiah 41:10 says, "Fear thou not; for I am with thee; Be not dismayed; for I am thy God: I will strengthen thee: yea I will Help thee: I will uphold thee with the right hand of my righteousness."

The Lord will provide a way of escape for us, but we must hold on and wait on Him. I think this stanza from a hymn, written by Jennie Wilson, says it best:

Hold Your Fire!

Time is filled with swift transition,
None on earth unmoved can stand.
Build your hopes on things eternal,
Hold to God's unchanging hand.

Nothing and no one can separate us from God's love and
eternal purpose. When we come to the point where we want
to quit, we must not! Instead, we should begin to praise God.
We may be in a pit, but we do not need to become pitiful in
our actions. We need to praise Him in the pit, with our mouth
open wide, and refuse to lose by announcing to the enemy: "I
am going to stand until the pit is passed, and my light is re-lit.
I will stand until the shaking quits and I feel peace again, until
my loneliness passes and my marriage is restored, until I am
out of debt and my struggle is over."

When Jeremiah was placed in his pit of persecution, he
was depressed, suicidal, and unhappy. His pilot light had gone
out. He had a break down of insight due to the lack of Son-
light. He had lost his passion (drive) and motivation (fire).
However, when he began to recall the goodness of the Father,
then his flame was rekindled with heavenly fire. In his pit he
found praise for God, his provider and deliver. Just before that,
out of his own mouth, Jeremiah admitted that he was never
again going to praise the name of God, but he said that there
was something in him that would not allow him to quit—
something that was just like fire shut up in his bones.

God sent Jeremiah relief through resurgence of his own
spirit. He reactivated his passion and lifted him from despair.
This brings to mind the scripture, "Count it all joy when ye
fall into divers temptations; knowing this, that the trying of
your faith worketh patience" (James 1:1-2. KJV). Child of
God, hold your fire!

Challenge 9
JEHOVAH ROPHE—
THE LORD OUR HEALER

Alerting—The Facts

Missing pieces: It can be plainly seen as Christians that our battles are not against other people but against the forces of darkness of this world. Satan and his demon cohorts are very real, and they are our worst enemies. In this battle, we cannot rely on human power and resources, but our security and victory will come as we stand against these spiritual enemies, wielding the spiritual weapons and clothed in the spiritual armor of the Lord God of host. Christ came to set the captives (those caught in the throws of sin) free. Anything that inhibits, hinders, or halts you from the divine plan to worship God is spiritual warfare (Eph. 2:2). If we're going to win the battle against the devil, we must (1) know who is the enemy (the devil), (2) have protection (the armor of God), and (3) possess power (the Holy Spirit).

Declaring—Your Role

According to the Bible, every Christian has the right and power to resist the devil and his attacks: "No weapon that is formed against thee shall prosper; and every tongue that shall rise against thee in judgment thou shalt condemn. This is the heritage of the servants of the Lord, and their righteousness is of me, saith the Lord" (Isaiah 54:17).

Activating—What Will You Do Now?

You must accept total mastership of Jesus in every area of

your life. Second, you must be willing to deal with the cross in your life. This must be an ongoing experience of total surrender (dying to self). Finally, you must learn to hear and obey the Lord as He speaks to your spirit.

———•••——

There's always a way
through the going rough,
and only your best is good enough;
you haven't the time
to count each loss,
so if the bridge is out,
swim across.

Chapter 10

What Is in Your House?

The wife of a man from the company of the prophets cried out to Elisha, "Your servant, my husband, is dead and you know that he revered the Lord. But now his creditor is coming to take my two sons as his slaves." Elisha replied to her, "How can I help you? Tell me, what do you have in your house?" (2 Kings 4: 1-3)

In this story, the woman's husband has died and left her destitute. Because of his untimely death, his unpaid bills became her inheritance. Her only assets were her two sons. The creditor was requiring her to present the sons as payment for the debt. The husband had been a committed servant of God and had served Elisha with excellence, so she brought her case to him because he was the head prophet.

We sometimes forget that God's provision is included in obedience. The purpose of a question is to provoke a thought, which will produce an action that will produce results. The gathering of vessels in this text is the indicator that there are insufficient funds in the house. What is in your house? What is available around you that can be used for the service of the Lord? Discovery is God's way of teaching us dependence upon Him. This is a lesson of faith! When you check your resources and come up empty, look to the Author of your faith. Reliance upon Him, for instance, should not occur only when you have gone to the bank and found that you are overdrawn on your account. Our dependence on Him should remain constant throughout our relationship with Him. The woman in the story is in transition. Her behavior indicates that her situation is serious.

When all resources are depleted, God will allow us to come into contact with someone who can put us in the direction of help. Elisha asked her what was in her house. Have you ever needed an answer, and all you received were more questions? When you are at the brink of disaster, the last thing that you want to hear is, "What are you going to do now?" Yet, often, this is exactly how God responds.

One sunny summer day when I was about seven years old, out of the blue, my father asked me what seven times seven was. I responded, "49." After thinking about it, I said, "Dad, you didn't know that?" But what I had not realized was that he was testing me. He was not asking the question because he had somehow forgotten the answer. My father wanted to know if I knew the answer.

Hide And Seek

In the book of Genesis, chapters 1 and 3, you will find the story of the rise and fall of our foreparents, Adam and Eve.

Disobedience plunged mankind into the ultimate recession from the provision of God. Adam and Eve became painfully aware of their plight and downfall in the Garden of Eden as they were forced from their paradise into obscurity. Their inability to be reinstated was even more painful. Their first response to their situation was to hide in shame from their Creator. Hide and Seek became their game.

We are all familiar with this one; it was a choice game of our childhood. The rules are simple. Two or more people participate. All but one run to find a hiding place. This one, who has been chosen and given the title "It," becomes the seeker who stays behind and counts to 10 while the players scurry for good hiding places before they hear It announce that he has reached 10. The object is to avoid being tagged and becoming It. There is a preselected safe area. If you can make it there and cry, "I'm safe," you cannot be tagged. Whoever became It, had to chase the other players in hopes of tagging one of them. Proverbs 18:10 says, "The name of the Lord is a strong tower: the righteous run into it, and is safe."

Adam and Eve did not hide themselves because they felt like humoring God. The shame of disclosure had forever changed their relationship with their heavenly Father. As usual, the Father came to the place in the garden where He had always found His children safely awaiting Him. Now it was empty, quiet, and uninviting. The Lord cried out as His voice walked throughout the garden, "Adam, where are you?" (Gen. 3:9) The voice of God had always been a pleasant one to Adam. Now His voice brought fear and startled them, causing them to hide out in bushes. God is all-knowing; certainly, He knew where they were. It was not a question of their geography; it was now a question of their spirituality.

What Is in Your House?

God called to notice the fact that we must know where we are. The widow in the text was requesting relief from her inherited responsibility. Has life ever given you a problem that you did not ask for? Have you found yourself in the place called Why Me? You are not alone. God has not somehow misplaced you. Know that He is calling you because He knows where you are. The loving voice of the Father is calling you into accountability. The decisions we make will affect the outcome of our destiny. Where are you? is a question of revelation, not speculation. When you leave the safe place and are tagged It by the enemy, Satan, you end up chasing things that are usually out of reach and out of bounds.

Elisha listened to the widow's complaint and responded, "What do you have in your house?" She replied, "All I have left in the house is a cruse of oil." In other words, all she had was leftovers.

God can do much with leftovers. Do you remember the young lad with just two fish and five loaves of bread? After Jesus touched and blessed the food, it fed 5,000 men, women, and children. Do you recall the woman with a handful of meal? Remember, she had planned to cook what she had left, then lie down and die. Instead, she first cooked a cake for the prophet, and God multiplied the leftover grain until the house was full. Elisha instructed the widow to go and borrow many vessels from her neighbors. She did so and brought them home, filling her house with empty vessels.

The Lord wants you to prepare for Him to release your increase. You cannot use what you have been using. For this next move of God, you are going to need fresh vessels. He instructed her to pour the oil she had left into the empty vessels until she ran out of oil. Oil is a symbol of the Holy Spirit. It is also a symbol of the anointing of God. The anointing of the Lord obliterates lack. He is going to change things for you. God is going to do three things for you.

1) *He is going to change time*—What took years to do will now take moments. Romans 9:28 says, "For He will finish the work and cut it short . . . ." Amos 9:13 says, "You'll be sowing with one hand and reaping with the other."

He will remove the doubt. Romans 8:28 says, "For all things work together for the good to them who love the Lord and are called according to his purpose." The difference between masterful and mediocre is focus!

2) *He will remove the enemy*—Exodus 14:13 says, "The Egyptians whom ye have seen today ye shall see them again no more forever."

3) *He will remove the lack*—Exodus 3:21 says, "And I will give this people favor in the sight of the Egyptians: and it shall come to pass. That, when ye go, ye shall not go empty."

I believe Elisha wanted this woman to give out of her want, and pour into that which was empty around her. God performs a miracle with a little bit. All God requires is a little bit of faith—the size of a mustard seed. The woman filled every vessel that she had borrowed and had oil to spare.

She was able to sell the vessels of oil, maintain the status of her household, pay her inherited debt, and have enough left to put away for later (money in the bank). I believe God wants us to look in our house (spiritual man) and find the remnant of oil. Faith is not credit; however, it does hide itself in the shadow of trust. Faith is trusting God with leftovers. It will become clear that, in spite of everything that has happened in your life, God is not finished with you, yet. There is more oil in you!

Challenge 10
JEHOVAH ELOHEENU—
THE LORD OUR GOD

Alerting—The Facts

When seeking a companion, the question is asked, who do I open to and who should I look for? In your loneliness and rejection, what does it profit you to reject the Lord our God? You complain of loneliness and that the spirit of rejection hounds you daily. Why? I know the reason you hunger for things is that you have sought the wrong companions and you are not satisfied. God says, "Can you listen for me? I want to abide in you, so we can be fully one. That means that I must be who you select for your true companion—the One you seek for solace and peace; the One you seek for learning, for growth and development; the One who puts a vital word in you so that it can be brought to fullness in what I have ordained for you, My yielded vessel. Do you know who I am? I am the author and finisher of your faith. Seek Me."

Declaring—Your Role

God says, "Remember who you are and that I have set before you an open door that no man can shut. Once you have walked through the open door, you will be walking on the sacred ground of destiny, sealed off from the hand of the enemy.

Remember that unless you abide in me, you can do nothing. I allow things in your life to make your inner temple a place I can call home."

Activating—What Will You Do Now?

God declares, "It is important to fill your heart, mind, and soul with me. That is my design for you. My sheep hear my voice. Be careful whom you let in My home, My abode, and My temple, for you are the temple of My Holy Spirit. It is My expectation that you will allow your will to be immersed in Mine. I am your sufficiency in all things, and as you dispense of the carnal and cleave to the supernatural, you will be satisfied in a way you cannot imagine. Be Mine. Be My companion. Be My abode. Surrender and be My temple, and I will give you joy."

Chapter 11

No Fire in the House

Where's the Heat?

One fall morning, I was awakened by frigid air unexpectedly filling my bedroom. I stirred for a few moments, to no avail, to find relief somewhere beneath my covers. The feeling remained the same—cold! As I lay there, the problem was getting worse as the temperature seemed to plunge even further. I could not understand the reason for this discomfort, because the weather forecast the day before had made no mention of exceptionally low temperatures coming during the night or the next morning, and I was surprised by the sudden change. After wrestling with the cold for a few minutes, I finally decided to get out of the bed and turn on the heat. As I walked into the hallway toward the thermostat, I could feel that the whole house was cold. While I was under the covers, I had no way of knowing that the rest of the household was probably just as miserable as I was, suffering the same discomfort from the cold. I turned the thermostat to the heat setting and listened for the familiar sound that indicates the furnace is on, but nothing happened. As I flipped the control on and off again, I was forced to realize that the problem was not in the thermostat's control. The problem was the furnace, the center of the heat source for the entire house.

The Holy Spirit provides the fire we need in our spiritual houses in the same way. Think of Him as the central factor for the heat that we need to fire us along through the discomforts of outside forces such as fear, stress, loneliness, and poor self-esteem. Our heavenly Father, through the Holy Spirit, provides the fire we need for our spiritual house.

If we are not prepared for the change these forces can bring, outside temperatures or forces will affect the temperature of our spirit man. The thermostat of the Holy Spirit should be heavily relied upon to offset any changes.

As I checked the furnace, what I had suspected became apparent. The pilot light to the furnace had gone out. The same can occur in our spiritual lives. When the Holy Spirit no longer has first place in our lives, we are cold. There is neither light nor life. The furnace is representative of our relationship with the Father. The house is symbolic of the temple that our spirit resides in. The pilot light is symbolic of our anointing, or in this case, our fire. When our pilot light is lit, we are warm, enabled, and functioning. We have purpose. However, when our light has gone out, we become cold, powerless, and unable to function—living yet not alive!

Get Back on Track

This section may not apply to you, so you may skip ahead to the next chapter if you wish. But for the benefit of those to whom God is talking right now, listen! If you want to dig deeper, or you're a person who needs to re-ignite your fire for God, then read on.

One of the purposes of the Holy Spirit is to keep us consistent in our Christian walk. No matter what our vocation or calling may be, we need the Holy Spirit to control your life. God does not want us to have a yo-yo type relationship with Him. For this reason, He gave us His precious Spirit to guide us into all truth (John 15). One of the essential elements in living for God is to follow His direction.

Re-igniting the pilot light (our anointing) is the only way to re-light the furnace (our relationship with the one and only true God) and receive heat. The cold that I experienced could have been averted if I had checked the furnace the night before. You see, I had not prepared for the change in the temperature outside. A good time for us to check your furnace is during the change of seasons.

In order to light the pilot, we must have fire from an outside source. The Holy Spirit is our outside source. Poor maintenance can lead to the pilot light going out. As life issues stack high upon us, we can lose our passion (drive) and motivation (fire) for ministry if we do not maintain our relationship with the Father.

Is your spiritual house cold because outside forces are weighing you down? Has your ministry experienced a set back, causing you to blame yourself and feel as though you have failed and can't move ahead? Are you struggling with being cold under the covers? The Seven Steps to Quality Devotions will help to put you back on track.

Seven Steps to Quality Devotions

Be Honest—Tell Him how you feel. No secrets can be kept from the Father.

Be Direct—He loves it when you come to Him.

Be Bold—Go to Him. Don't be ashamed, He loves you.

Listen Carefully—He cares. Focus on Him as He speaks to you.

Have an Attitude of Gratitude—Be grateful to Him.

Obey His Voice—It shows that you honor Him.

Be Thankful—Think of His goodness toward you.

Praise Him for Everything You Have!

Does Anybody Have a Light?

The Lord is my light and my salvation whom shall I fear, the Lord is the strength of my life of whom shall I be afraid (Psalm 27:1).

The most important thing about bringing you aflame again is the permanence of it. Mark the source. You should not take lightly who, or what, you are re-ignited by, because it will determine the consistency of your walk. The question of your eternal nature will be answered with your choice of source. Does it have a consistent nature? Is it eternal? If the answer to either question is an emphatic no, then you must question if you can live with that kind of firepower in your life. You don't want to be burned alive by the very thing that is supposed to ignite your solemn spirit again.

You were once dead in spirit, in joy, and in attitude. Don't make the same mistake again. This is your life. This is your ministry. You must use prayerful discretion when choosing your source of reconnection.

At the gravesite of Dr. Martin Luther King, Jr., in Atlanta, Georgia, there burns an eternal flame. This means, of course, that the flame does not go out, no matter the severity of the weather. This flame burns under the condition that the natural gas, which is its source, will not become depleted. If it does, the flame will no longer be eternal. As long as the gas gives life to that flame, it will continue to burn. There is a revelatory difference in how God's supply works. It does so without any limitations whatsoever. Neither strikes nor embargoes, not sanctions or any outside force or power can extinguish the fire of God. He has unlimited resources and needs no reserves. God's faithfulness will never fail us. "In the beginning God created the heaven and the earth . . . And God said, let there be light: and there was light" (Genesis 1:1-3).

God is the creator of fire and the initiator of light. The Bible says, "For the Lord thy God is a consuming Fire . . ." (Duet. 4:24). The fire of God not only anoints us but it also gives light to those who follow it. The Bible says, "And the Lord went before them by day in a pillar of cloud, to lead them the way; and by night in a pillar of fire, to give them light; to go by day and night (Exod. 13:21).

The Lord would not have you wandering in a directionless circle. The light of the Lord will guide you every step of the way. The Word of God also says, "He took not away the pillar of cloud nor the pillar of fire from before the people." So whether you are in a seemingly endless night or moving about in an uneventful day, He will be there when you need Him.

God is the only true source of light, so put away any futile searching into other sources. His credentials are impeccable. The Bible testifies that from everlasting to everlasting, He is God. There is no beginning or ending in Him. Who else can say that! He loves you unconditionally. His mercy toward us is staggering in comparison to anything else. There is none like Him. Let Him completely illuminate your soul, mind, and body. Only then will you be able to proclaim, "Yes! I have light, the light of the world!"

The Upper Room

And when the day of Pentecost was fully come they were all with one accord in one place and suddenly there came a sound from Heaven as of a rushing mighty wind, and it filled all the house where they were sitting (Acts 2:1-2).

When God fills our house, He anoints us with power and purpose. In the Old Testament, the anointing was placed on places, things or people. In Genesis 28:18, we see the account of Jacob anointing the city of Luz, which was about 10 miles

North of Jerusalem and 60 miles North of Beersheba—where Jacob had left his family for fear that his brother Esau would kill them. Rising early on the morning after his encounter with God, he took the stone that he had used as a pillow and set it up as a pillar and poured oil on top of it.

Jacob anointed the area as a blessed place. To commemorate the occasion of the Lord appearing to him, Jacob changed the name from Luz (to turn aside) to Bethel (house of God). This is a clear message for us today that says after we are anointed, some things should change inside of us. We should change! Our attitude toward our season does change. When our vision is greater, our insight will increase.

Finally, our faith should be stronger because the Lord has spoken to us. Jesus said, "My sheep know my voice and a stranger they will not follow" (John 10:4-5). Sheep are led; goats are driven. How about that! Sheep will follow only their shepherd. Christ is our Shepherd, and He leads us into green pastures (consistent provision) and beside the still waters (stability and peace).

God not only anoints places, as we have seen, but He also anoints objects and people. The Hebrew word *mashach* means "to rub in." The Greek word *chrism* means to "to smear." In Israel, the insect population was so bad that a shepherd had no choice but to exercise a mashach and chrism method to bring relief to his sheep. He had to anoint (smear) the sheep with oil for their protection. The insects that had been biting the sheep became bogged down in the oil and could no longer irritate the sheep. If the sheep were not anointed, the insects would continue to torment the sheep with stinging bites, leaving them with sores and infection.

Christ Jesus, the anointed one, is our good Shepherd, who

will not hesitate to rub on, and smear on, the anointing He has designated for us. We do not have to suffer from the irritation of being bitten, which leaves us with open wounds in our hearts and minds—wounds which can become infected over time.

As leaders in the kingdom of God, we must realize that we need the anointing of God to survive while on this earth until Jesus comes. Without Him, we can do nothing. The trauma and drama of life will make us conclude that Jesus is the answer! If we are honest, we will confess that we cannot walk a victorious life without becoming empowered by the Holy Spirit.

Take Me to That Place

The upper room is a place of worship, and worship brings relief and release. The Upper Room was set aside for the sole purpose of worshiping the Lord God. Any place where you set yourself with determination to seek God's presence and find it is an upper room; it is a place where all things come together. Every believer should have such a place. Ambiance is not something you should focus on; the place is not for show and tell. Usually, it is not an elaborate or elegant place. It is simply a place where the Lord will meet you. Jesus commanded the disciples to tarry in the Upper Room until they were endowed, or filled, with His Holy Ghost power. Take me to that place where all pretenses are absent and prestige is not sought after!

We have been divided for too long. If we are going to have intimacy with the Father and fellowship with each other, then the reformation of our worship of God is critical. I'm speaking to the Body of Christ—the Church, the Bride of Christ. For the world to believe that we are serious about God, we have to lay aside separate but equal religion and walk together to the upper room. The power that we need to love one another is in the upper room!

How can we say to other cultures and nations that our God is a God of unity and that His house is for all people while we remain in a posture that we can't, or won't, worship together?

When God selects someone for service, color is not a consideration. God does not see color; He sees character. The Lord takes us to that place where we can be filled. One hundred and twenty believers came together and assembled in one place for one purpose—to be filled with the Holy Spirit. They were sent to receive power. They were not called because of status or pure repute, but because of the desires of their hearts. I don't know who made up the invitation list, but I'm sure it was not man-made. When God calls us, it is always to a designated spot. Just as He told Elijah that the raven would feed him at the chosen place, so, too, God chooses the place. He sets the time. He makes up the menu. We go.

The 120 were there to be ignited with an unquenchable fire, a fire of unlimited resources, a fire that would fill the emptiness within. After 10 days in the Upper Room (God worked out some things in them before He put something in them), suddenly, there was a sound as that of a mighty rushing wind. The anointing has a sound, and it is quick and powerful, unlike any other sound. He is distinct. He is quick, strong, and noticeable, moving while taking over with sudden power that loudly says, "Whoosh." God is present! The Bible says, "He filled the entire house where they were . . . " God does a complete work. He leaves no area unaffected and no stone unturned. All that we yield to Him, He will fill. The anointing produces fire in us. The Word says, "And then appeared unto them cloven tongues like of fire . . . " (Acts 2:3).

Even though the anointing is not actual physical fire, its properties have the same character in that it consumes the old ill-productive things in us and brands us anew. The passion, motivation, and power of fire are tools (evidence) of the anointing. When God sends His Spirit, the anointing will be present. Allow God to fill your house today. Don't let it be said of you that there is no fire in your house. From the hollow of your emptiness, tell the Lord, "Fill my house!" I had an uncle whom I lovingly referred to as Uncle Champ, who told me a story many years ago. I don't even know if the following story was true, but it will help me to illustrate my final point.

It's Cold in Here!

The winters in Youngstown, Ohio, were brutal. A major contributor was the cold, northern air that rushed across Lake Erie to come and settle in on us. This moving air had to travel only about 60 miles to engulf Youngstown in all its winter glory. As a young boy, I remember the temperatures dropping to below zero, and that was considered normal.

My Uncle Champ told me that one cold morning about 2:00 a.m., my grandfather shouted from his bedroom for his son Phillip to go into the basement and check the coal furnace because the house had become cold. (This often took place during the 50s and 60s, when coal furnaces were common.) Coal was stored in a bin next to their furnace. When they needed heat, one of them tossed a few shovels full into the furnace. But after some time had lapsed—enough time for the house to have become warm again—the house was still cold.

" Phillip!" shouted my grandfather. "Did you check the fire in the furnace?"

"Yes," he replied.

"Well, how is it?"

After a long pause, Phillip shouted, "It's out!"

Well, you can imagine what happened to Phillip. My grandfather's asking Phillip to check the fire in the furnace is the same as the Lord asking Adam, where are you? When Phillip answered "It's out," it was the same as Adam's response, "Lord this woman you gave me . . ." (Gen. 3:12). They were excuses to hide the obvious. They allowed the fire to go out, diminish, and die.

Your might think that Phillip was not responsible for this task in the first place. Yes, he was. Although he was not the originator of the fire on that day, he was the maintenance person for it. He was sent to check the fire. He found it dwindling but did nothing.

Out of his state of being cold, the "taste" of warmth under his covers became his temporary love, over and above obeying the request of his father. And due to that one action, the whole house was cold, upsetting the comfort, and possibly the health, of everyone in it. Adam was at fault, too. He allowed his fire to be taken because of disobedience.

Dear reader, pastor, church elder, layman, and all who make up the Body of Christ, take a STEP to strive toward expected provision. Do not let laziness or idleness or the issues of life put out your fire that prompts you to work, to minister, and to change the lives of others.

Challenge 11
JEHOVAH HOSEENU—
THE LORD OUR MAKER

Alerting—The Facts

The glasshouse. Why do we live in glass houses and love to throw stones? Our nature is such that a break of any sort could be devastating. Is it presumptuous to say that? Most of us go from day to day with only minor ripples of conflict in our path; others have major ones. It is in the times when turbulence hits that we wonder, Will our glass house survive the blow? Can you take a hit and recover? Reality is sometimes too deep for words. However, I believe you and I we were put on earth to add something to it. Nobody notices a broken doll in a toy manufacturing plant, where they make new dolls every minute. The glass house is where we are so careful about everything, but we never do much of anything. We just survive, exist, and take up space. From embryo to maturity—from beginning to end—we should bring something to the table of life that has value.

Declaring—Your Role

We are the children of a God who has gone to every extent to let us know that He cares about every hair on our heads and that He hears every prayer. We can cast our cares upon Him, for He cares for us. He wants, above all things, that we prosper and be in health, even as our soul prospers. God sent the living Word, Jesus, who was, and is, "a man of sorrows acquainted with Grief" (Isa. 53:3) and is a redeemer sent by God because of His love for us. God perfects all that concerns us.

Activating—What Will You Do Now?

Jesus gave me a little light; I'm going to let it shine. Jesus gave me a little light, and I'm going to let it shine. Jesus gave you a little light, and you're going to let it shine. Let it shine. Let it shine. Let it shine! Even a tiny candle makes a difference.

Chapter 12

God Is Our Rock

As I write today I am in need of prayer. Imagine that, a pastor in need of prayer! Nevertheless, I am. There are some who actually believe that pastors never need prayer. Wrong! We need it more than most. As a matter of fact, a pastor cannot function without a daily allotment of uncontested, steady, earnest, uninhibited, hanging-it-all-out-there prayer. Very recently, I specifically asked the Lord to have one of my intercessors call me because things were going downhill and I needed an answer. Within hours, God did just that. They called. I am better. God is faithful. Thank you, Lord!

This is meaningful because the enemy really wants to stop the message God has given us. But you know what, God may not answer you as quickly as He answered me on that day. To tell the truth, many times He hasn't. But I always ask, because to me, He's Dad. I'm simply saying that God is our rock in times of trouble. He's a solid foundation to lean on.

Do you remember the story of David and Goliath? Some of us learned the story in Sunday school. David was a shepherd boy, small in stature and handsome to look upon. He was from a family of eight boys, and he had one sister. He was considered by some of his brothers to be cocky and loquacious. A year came when war broke out in his country.

Three of his brothers had already received their reporting orders from the king's dispatch, but because David was too young to be drafted, he had to remain at home to watch the sheep. One day, his father, Jesse, asked him to take some lunch to his brothers who were fighting. Obediently, he did so.

As he approached the camp, he noticed that all the fighters were standing around watching and listening to a giant named Goliath. I can imagine this giant was cussing and fussing, flinging strings of insulting expletives that are not to be repeated! He was launching one irreverent look after another. *Who is this Nemesis?* David wondered inwardly. Then he asked the others, "Who is this man that you should allow him to offend our God?" David was no trained warrior, but he was a born fighter, so he postured himself for the fight of his young life.

David was not a scholar nor was he renown. He had no Franklin Planner that held his schedule on neatly written lines, no reference points to look to so that he could accomplish his daily appointments. He had no Internet access. For him, there was no business plan available that charted shepherd boys, and there was no martial arts training either. He was a shepherd boy facing a bully. Goliath was a known murderer, a paid mercenary who was trained in gorilla warfare. Some of the notches in his belt came about by default; just from the sight of him men quit, turned, and ran away. Goliath had weapons of iron and brass, and his coat of mail, which weighed about 125 pounds, was massive and intimidating.

The head of one of his spears weighed about 15 pounds. And to top it off, he was 9 feet 9 inches tall, boastful, and arrogant. To make things even worse, he had many people to cheer him on. David on the other hand, did not have much on his resume. David braved himself to tell King Saul, against his brother's orders, that he would fight Goliath. David gave the king his business card that read, "David, son of Jesse. I have personally killed one bear and one lion through hand-to-hand combat. I trust God and am willing to fight!" King Saul offered his personal armor to David to wear while he fought Goliath, but David protested, " I cannot fight with this, I have not proved it. I only need what God has given me to win this fight" (1 Sam. 17:39). Though David's family would not cheer him on, he fought anyway.

Against the odds, fight anyway; when ridiculed, fight anyway; if outmatched, fight anyway; when you have no advantages, fight anyway. The battle is not yours; it's the Lord's. God knows what we need and where we are. Because we are creatures of time and space, we are pinned in. But even so, time and space has no barrier for God because He is infinite; God dwells in the eternal now. He is everywhere at the same time, and there is nothing He does not know. Don't believe it? Just ask Ezekiel.

In the story of the dry bones, God asked Ezekiel, "Can these bones live?" He responded, "Lord God, you know wether or not they can live" (Eze. 37:3). God knows what we need. If God knows the ways of the eagles and the mighty oceans, if He can hear the whisper of every brook and gentle breeze, if God knows the way of the whales in the sea and even the fish in your aquarium, if God knows the number of hairs on your head and the number of cells in your body, if God can give you over 200 bones and build your skeletal system with them and give you over 500 muscles to hold it all together, then certainly He can fight every one of your battles. Let me tell you what I heard a friend of mine say about our God:

No tyrant can frighten Him
No congress can impeach Him
No army can subdue Him
No power can subdue Him
No surprise can come to Him
No distance is beyond Him
No height is above Him
No depths are below Him
No contemporaries with Him
No peers beside Him
No deceiver can deceive Him!

God is too truthful to lie and too strong to be defeated. He is too omnipresent to be absent. Our God is too watchful to sleep and too concerned to be negligent. The Lord is too stable be moved and too steadfast to fail. He's too good to be mean and too loving not to care. What I like about God is that He doesn't have to travel because He is Jehovah Shama. He is already there. Wherever you need Him, there he will be! He knows your intentions, your habits, your heart, your mind, and He is acquainted with all your ways. He knows your name and your number. He knows all your strengths and all your weakness. He knows the good and the bad. He knows it all.

There is also another message in this story. David was a

boy. God could have permitted this fight to be held after he became a man, or even when he was king. God could have placed another strong warrior against Goliath, but he didn't. I believe He didn't because God wanted to show us that a shepherd boy, armed with no other weapons but the name of his God and five smooth rocks, could overcome if he would faint not. To subdue the mighty, God often uses those who are among the least likely to succeed.

Five Stones

Why five stones? I can't say that I know for sure. Some say it was because five is the number of grace. Others speculate that Goliath had four brothers and God had David prepared for all of them in case they took revenge.

What I do know is that I, too, have been in a fight with an arrogant, egotistical bully who sold wolf tickets to me, and had a large crowd to egg him on. The crowd was armed to the teeth and had no doubt that Goliath would win the day. I, too, have had well-meaning friends, who, themselves, fainted at the sight of a bully. There have been even wiser friends who were "kings" in my life and advised me not to fight. But I fought anyway.

Just as David did, we all have stood on mountains having a valley in between. Many times, we have had to cross the valleys to win a victory. But why five stones? I believe that the first stone was **Faith**, for without faith it is impossible to please God. Further, faith is the substance of things we hope for and the evidence of things we do not see. When all that is between you and your victory is a big drop, you naturally look down. Carnal men do not naturally comprehend spiritual things. Proverbs says the heart of a king is in the hand of the

Lord, and He will turn it whithersoever He will. The second stone is **Hope**. Hope deferred makes the heart sick. If a man sees the victory, what does he yet hope for?

The third stone is the **Word of God**. "Lead me to the rock that is higher than I " (Psalm 61:2). Upon a rock, the church was built. Jesus is the rock in a weary land. Revelation says, "His name shall be called the Word of God" (Rev. 19:13). For the Word was made flesh, and dwelt among us. The fourth stone must be **Love**. "For he that loveth not, knoweth not God, for God is Love" (1 John 4:7-8). The fifth stone is **Tenacity**. Do not give up no matter what your situation may be! We walk by faith and not by sight, but we have to stick to the battle. Remember the woman who sought after her master until He blessed her (Luke 18:1-5).

With these same stones, you, too, can defeat your Goliaths. Don't be afraid to use them. Wield them with your spiritual strength! Your Goliaths will be easy to identify. They will always stand between you and your breakthrough. The battle will always be intense, but don't worry and don't look down. You have five smooth stones for your Goliath, and they are all powerful. Also, remember that "God has not given us a spirit of fear, but of power of love and of a sound mind" (2 Tim 1:7).

If you were to get a package in the mail with no return address, before you opened it, wouldn't you question where it came from? If the spirit of fear were to plague you, would not you ask the question, if the Lord didn't send it, who did? Once you discover the answer, the floodgates of peace will overwhelm your soul. Challenges will come, but we have a Chancellor who will cancel all confusion, because God is Faithful. God is Our Rock!

Challenge 12
JEHOVAH TSIDKEENU— THE LORD OUR RIGHTEOUSNESS

Alerting—The Facts

I'm fragile, handle with care. I believe in my sometimes-fragile heart that God wants me to trust in Him so that I will take the next step. I remember when my father was teaching me to trust him. One day he told me to stand at the top of the stairs—about five steps away, which seemed like 50 to me. He said, "Jump. I will catch you." At first I said, "No way, Dad!" However, he insisted it would be OK. After much prompting, I finally jumped, and he caught me. I never doubted Dad again. That is an example of how it is with God. He is saying jump into My will. Trust me; I won't let you fall. Perhaps sometimes we will falter in faith or stumble in strength, but he'll be right there. He promised!

Declaring—Your Role

Remember this: your worst days are never so bad that you are beyond the reach of God's grace, and your best days are never so good that you are beyond the need of God's love. No matter how much your enemies try this year, they will not succeed. You have been destined to make it, and you shall surely achieve all your goals this year. Victory and prosperity will be coming to you in abundance. Today God has confirmed the end of your sufferings, sorrows, and pains, because He that sits on the throne has remembered you. He has taken away the hardships and given you joy. He will never let you down.

Activating—What Will You Do Now?

Forget those who may have pointed or been curious over the years. Forget those who wounded you instead of encouraging you. Bless God for the ones who cared enough to pray for you, who had you on their minds. Bless the souls who offered help when it seemed that no one cared. Bless God for intercessors who keep lifting us up in prayer. Give thanks unto the Lord, for He is good.

Chapter 13

Lift Up Your Head

Mr. Squirrel

As I write these words today, my mind and spirit are in conflict. I sit in my den, watching a squirrel in my backyard. He is carrying a walnut from my tree to his home. While watching it, I notice how frequently he stops and looks up and around. *Why?* I ask myself. *Why is he stopping so often?* He picks up the walnut, walks a few squirrel steps, puts the nut down, lifts up his head, and looks around, almost as though there were an invisible traffic light in my backyard controlling his actions. For him, what should have been just a 30-second trip has turned into a 20-minute journey.

I move from my chair to the door to get a closer view, and I see why Mr. Squirrel is being so cautious. Across the road is a pack of dogs. They have been patrolling the neighborhood for food. And while they seem not to be paying him any attention, the squirrel is watching every move they make. If it seems to him that the dogs are advancing or drifting too closely to him, then he drops his walnut snack and looks up to investigate their exact location. I wonder, if he has enough God-given sense to look up, then why don't we? Why is it that when problems or persecution comes, we walk around with our heads down, our hearts down, and our attitudes down? We walk around with a down-in-the-mouth look. I believe the Lord was trying to tell us something.

The hounds of life will sneak up on us if we are not observant. You see, we can be so engrossed in the immediate that we fail to watch and pray.

The adversary, the devil, like a roaring lion, goes to and fro seeking whom he may devour. Status won't protect you from this enemy. Money won't buy him off. As children of the King, we must realize he wants to steal, kill, and destroy us. When Jesus came from the Jordan River after His baptism by John the Baptist, the Spirit drove him into the wilderness, where He was to be tempted by Satan. After a series of tests—the test of need (turn these stones into bread), the test of greed (I will give you all of this), and the test of recognition (bow down and worship me)—Jesus totally rebuked the adversary and was victorious. Matthew 4:11 says that angels came and ministered unto Him to strengthen Him. When Jesus was in trouble, He looked up. He depended on His Father for answers. I'm not saying that the squirrel prayed when he looked up, but on the other hand, if God could make a mule talk, then He could have a squirrel pray? Hmm.

If I was Mr. Squirrel in that situation, I believe I would have prayed, "Lord, I'm trying to take this walnut home, but there is a chance that one of these dogs may see me and try to hurt me. You know I'm no match for them, and if one of them comes, they'll all come. So, Lord, if you don't mind, I need Your help and guidance to get home. Once I'm home, I'll be safe. The dogs won't be able to get me once I'm home. Thank you, Lord. Amen."

That reminds me of a story I heard many years ago. Two pilots were flying a shipment of cobra snakes from South America to a zoo in New York. The snakes were placed in crates and secured in the cargo bin, but during the take off, the latch on one of the crates came loose. In mid-flight, one of the snakes, looking for warmth, worked its way up to the cockpit.

As the snake poised itself to strike the pilot, the co-pilot told him not to move because one of the cobras was loose. The co-pilot radioed back to base and informed them of the situation. Base contacted a snake specialist to get help. The base called back and asked the co-pilot what their current altitude was. He informed them that the plane was about 10,000 feet above sea level. They were instructed to climb to 15,000 feet and report on the activity of the cobra once they had reached that altitude. When they reached 15,000 feet, the co-pilot reported that the snake was bobbing and weaving. Base instructed them to climb to 22,000 feet and report back. When they reached 22,000 feet, the co-pilot said, "The snake appears to have fallen asleep. What should I do?" Base replied, "The snake is incapacitated. Put it back in cage." The pilot and co-pilot did not know that the snake was a low-altitude creature. The higher they flew, the weaker it became. God wants us to know that when we belong to Him, our adversary, the devil (the snake), no longer has the ability to hurt or control our actions. The higher we go in God, the less of an effect he will have upon us.

Look Up. It's OK.

It's not that Satan can't threaten us with temptation, but when he does, Jesus has already provided a way of escape for us. If Mr. Squirrel can look up, so can you! Lift up your heads! Oh ye saints of the Most High. Lift up your heads! Be encouraged! Stand strong and hold on! Psalms 24:9-10 says it best:

> *Lift up your Heads, O ye gates; even lift them up, ye everlasting doors; and the King of glory shall come in. Who is this King of glory? The Lord of hosts, He is the King of glory.*

Regret and isolation can cause us to feel discouraged about our lives. When we have done our best and come up short, life can be lonely. Feelings of remorse can engulf our spirit as we rehearse the failures of the past. John was such a man: the cousin of Jesus; the forerunner of Christ's ministry; a preacher in the wilderness proclaiming to the world, "Behold the Lamb of God Who taketh away the sins of the world" (John 1:29).

John was called to baptize unto repentance, but the Lord Jesus was the Savior of the world. John's message was one of deliverance from bondage. Yet, even though he was committed and anointed to proclaim His message, he was imprisoned for doing so. From his cell of solitude, he wondered how his ministry had taken a turn for the worse. Have you ever felt like that? I have! I have found that I can love God with all my heart and still have to face trials. As Christians, we can be Spirit-filled and still encounter stress and worry as they try to sneak into our hearts.

Is Christ really who He says He is, or shall I look for another? You can be in ministry and somehow wonder, did you miss God? God never told you that the indicator for successful ministry was everything always being OK because it's just not true. There will be struggles, but God will not forsake you. He will send you a message through a sermon or a song. He'll allow someone to call you and pray for you in the midnight hour. Yes, even when you feel locked-up and locked-out, Jesus knows, and He is the source of your deliverance.

So I encourage you today, as John's disciples encouraged him, by saying, "Jesus told us to tell you, the blind receive their sight, and the lame walk, the leapers are cleansed, and the deaf Hear. The dead are raised up, and the poor have the gospel preached to them. And blessed is he whosoever shall not be offended [ashamed] in me" (Matt 11:4-6). Your living is not in vain. Your preaching is not in vain. Your ministry is not in vain. Your destiny is not in vain. Nothing can stop children of destiny. Deuteronomy 11:12 says, "The eyes of the Lord are always upon thee, from the beginning of the year even unto the end of the year."

This means that we are never out of the sight of our God. No matter what is ahead, He'll be there from beginning to end. So, lift up your head. God sees you and will help you in the times of trouble.

Closing Challenge
THE OMEGA

Alerting—The Facts

Feeling a void in your spirit? The enemy wants us to relax, or quit, our pursuit of God's will. He wants us to sacrifice our purity for carnality. In addition, he will wage this attack when situations in your life that you have believed God for are not changing and nothing is moving. The Bible says in Hebrews, "Don't let go of your confidence" (Heb.. 3:6). The enemy wants you to become bitter over the circumstances in your life so that a wedge will be placed between you and the Father. Nevertheless, your heavenly Father says, "Greater is he that is in you, than he that is in the world" (1 John 4:4). God said it, and that settles it!

Declaring—Your Role

Don't settle for the pain, poverty, or problems the devil offers you. During seasons of delay or periods of pause, endure, knowing your heavenly Father has everything in control. Maintain your purity before God. Don't cuss and fuss like a person with no hope. Trust God; He will perform what He has spoken.

Activating—What Will You Do Now?

Dan 11:32 says, "And by smooth words he will turn to godlessness those who act wickedly toward the covenant, but the people who know their God will display strength and do exploits". Therefore, friend, walk out in faith and watch the Lord make a spectacle out of the enemy. God respects His Word.

IN CONCLUSION

My prayer is that something I have said has struck your heartstrings, and that you are more encouraged and excited than before.

It is my prayer that something in this book made you search the Scriptures more, or you saw something in the spirit that you had not seen before. I pray there was a paragraph, a sentence, or even one word that helped you in some way. If so, my desire and mission for this book is complete.

God bless you in your walk with the Master.

DISCUSSION GUIDE

This guide is designed to provoke you, the reader, to search the Scripture for nuggets of faith. Like the gold miners of the early Gold Rush days would say, "There's gold in them there hills." Well, I would like to amend that by saying, "There's gold in the Word of God."

There will be two sections in the guide. In the first section, *Thoughts to Target*, you will find excerpts from each chapter to discuss. The second section, *Searching the Scriptures*, will help readers to dig deeper into the Word of God while researching the issues outlined for group discussion.

Chapter One—Fire Anyone?

Thoughts to Target
• The Word of God is our standard as Christian believers. Will you stick to your guns in a society of ever-changing morality?
• What does it cost to be anointed? How do you know when you're successful in ministry?
• If fire is a symbol of the Holy Spirit, should the passion in ministry be lacking today?
• Why does God choose people He knows will make mistakes?
• Have you ever been caught at the altar of public opinion? Why does God want us to be empowered by the Holy Spirit?

Search the Scriptures
• Read Jeremiah 20:9. Why was Jeremiah so hurt? What provoked him to worship God in spite of his situation?
• Read Hebrews 4:12. What does the Word of God do to our heart?
• Read Act's 2:1-17. How does the Holy Spirit manifest Himself today? How does the Holy Spirit help us in our day-to-day lives?
• Read Proverbs 3:5-6. How does this passage relate to you?
• Read Psalms 34:7. Did you feel God's presence today?

Chapter Two—Tanners

Thoughts to Target
• Do you know any tanners?
• I believe God wants someone He can trust to minister to His people. How do you feel about this statement?
• What qualities do you look for in leadership? Are they valid requirements?
• I think it's significant that God uses the least likely people to do his work. How do you feel about this?
• If your closest friend were God, would He have chosen you to do the work you're doing now, knowing what He knows about you? Discuss the way in which God called you into service.

Search the Scriptures
• Read 1 Samuel 16:7. Why do you think Samuel thought Eliab was God's best choice? Does God know our strengths as well as our weakness?

- How does God let you know you're His choice?
- Read John 15:16. Is it important that the Lord chose us?
- Through what does God promise to produce?
- Do you see fruit in your life?

Chapter Three—Images

Thoughts to Target

- How does your image of yourself help or hinder your walk with Christ?
- Do you agree that position with God is not a matter of placement, but of order?
- Describe your position with Jesus at this time.
- Would you have walked on the water if Jesus had called you?
- What is your motive for serving God?
- Under pressure, would you deny Jesus Christ as your Savior?
- Have you ever been AWOL in your ministry?
- According to John 15:16, how does God feel about you?
- I believe when God views us, He looks at us from the perspective of what we will become, so God never sees us where we are. God see us in His sovereign will, where we are blessed, powerful overcomers. How do you feel about this statement?
- Do you ever question the timing of events in your life?
- In a group discussion, discuss how you feel about God using a person whom you may not agree with.

Search the Scriptures
- Read Proverbs 3:1-5. How do you feel about it?
- Read Psalms 30:5. How long will the favor of God last in your life?
- Read Luke 9:37. How has the power of faith been demonstrated in your life?
- Read Isaiah 6:8. If God were to command you to work for Him, would you leave everything and go?

Chapter Four—Mine Only Son

Thoughts to Target
- What keeps us from letting God be Lord of our lives?
- Developing in God means total release and surrender to God. Do you agree?
- What do you feel the work of the kingdom is?
- Why is it impossible to please God without faith?
- Faith acts obediently to the commandments of God and lives victoriously in the blessings from God. Do you agree?
- Bishop Greenwood made a statement that deliverance is a powerful restorer of faith. How do you feel about this statement?
- Considering Moses' encounter with God, what stands out the most in your mind about it? Bishop Greenwood stated the purpose of the burning bush was not to give off heat, but to produce vision. Explain your feelings.

Search the Scriptures
- Read Genesis 1:1-27. Have you seen the Holy Spirit at

work in your life? Do you feel God has made you to serve Him? Explain.
- What do you learn from reading these passages?
- Read Heb. 11:1. The risky thing about faith is it means trusting God while walking with a blindfold on. How do you feel about this statement?
- Read Proverbs 29:2. What is so powerful about the righteous being in authority?

Chapter Five—Becoming of Age

Thoughts to Target
- Do you agree that God can use anyone, at any age?
a. How do you know if God is calling you to ministry?
b. Does God order your steps? Explain?
- Balanced faith means "being well rounded in all areas of your spirit." How do you as a believer accomplish this?
- As you develop in God, how should your faith change?
- How does the Holy Spirit help raise your awareness of His presence in times of trauma?
- God called David in his teens. Would you obey the voice of a person younger than yourself?

Search the Scripture
- Read John 2:6-8. Does God still perform miracles? In these passages do you see the magnitude of God's power? Explain?
- Read Psalms 118:8. How do you feel about this passage? How does confidence in God relate to trusting man?
- The Lord requires a willing vessel and a committed be-

liever. Why does God place so much emphasis on commitment?

• Read Joshua 1:1-3. What does crossing the Jordan mean to you? Why is it important for you to cross your Jordan?

• Read Joshua 3:10. When you don't sense the presence of God, faith must fill the gap between what you see and whom you know. Do you agree with this statement?

• Read 1 Peter 2:9. Were you surprised that God sees you as a royal priesthood? Out of all the people in the world, why do you think the Lord selected you for service?

Chapter Six—Lead Me, Guide Me

Thoughts to Target

• Have you ever been in a struggle between your will and God's purpose for your life? Who won?

• Do you think it is easy to follow God?

• Describe a situation when God led you by His Spirit.

• In what way did God reveal Himself to you?

Search the Scripture

• Read Hebrews 11:27. Moses endured because he saw Him who is invisible. How was this possible? In your group discussion talk about having endurance in Jesus.

• Read Daniel 6:3-4. Explain the spirit of excellence and what it does.

Chapter 7—You Can't Turn Back Now!

Thoughts to Target
- When serving God, why is retreat risky? Explain.
- Confidence is triumph dressed incognito. How do you feel about this statement? Have you ever wanted to resign from God's army, but He provoked you to re-enlist?
- What do you think Bishop Greenwood means by the statement "Guidance and protection are trademarks of our God"?
- Why does our adversary use fear against us? Do we have any weapons against fear? Explain.
- Has God promised to help us when we are under attack? How does God speak to you in times of conflict?

Search the Scripture
- Read Hebrews 11:34. Can you discuss periods when God quenched the violence in your life?
- Read John 10:10. Our adversary wants to inflict major damage upon us. Explain how we can counteract this attack?
- Read Act's 1:8. Explain some of the benefits of having the Holy Spirit inside of you.
- Read Isaiah 54:17. The Bible says, "No weapon formed against us shall prosper." Explain why they won't prosper.

Chapter 8—Whom Do You Resemble?

Thoughts to Target
- Why is it important for you to know who Jesus is? "You will never progress without sacrifice." How do you feel about this statement?

- How do you explain the disciples not understanding the true identity of Jesus?
- Have you ever struggled with the reality of who Jesus was in your life?
- When people see you, is it apparent who your spiritual Father is?

Search the Scripture
- Read Matthew 16:13-17. Why did Jesus question His disciples?
- Read Matthew 17:5. How would you respond if God spoke to you out of a cloud?
- Read Luke 17:20-21. Give an example of how you relate to the kingdom being within you.
- Read 2 Timothy 1:6. How do you, on a daily basis, stir up the gift of God that is in you?
- Read Isaiah 43:5-7. Explain why you were created. Who should get the glory out of your life?

Chapter 9—Hold Your Fire

Thoughts to Target
- When there is conflict in your spirit, it will cause you to alter your direction and dictate the wrong course of action. Have you ever felt this way?
- Do you agree that despair can leave you stripped of all dignity? Why?
- Choose one word that describes how you feel about having the favor of God upon your life.

1. Realize your greatness in God.
2. God's promises are yours by faith.
3. Get a vision from God and work it.
4. Go forth knowing the Lord is with you.
5. Claim confidence in Christ.
6. The Word shall not depart from you.
7. Go now and possess the land!

Search the Scripture
- Read Jeremiah 20:9. Has your faith ever been staggered in the manner described in this passage? If yes, how did you rebound from it?
- Read Psalm 34:19. Does this scripture change your view of afflictions?
- Read Isaiah 41:10. When was the last time you were in a fix and God strengthened you?
- Read James 1:1-2. What does James tell us to do in this passage? Can this really be done? How?

Chapter 10—What's in Your House?

Thoughts to Target
- Will God ever require you to do something you cannot do?
- Bishop Greenwood says that God's provision is included in your obedience to Him. How do you feel about this statement? Is God's provision always available to His children?
- Has God ever told you to wait? How did you respond to His answer?

- What is available around you that can be used for the service of the Lord?
- Does God expect you to yield yourself for His service?
- Can you identify anything in your spiritual or secular life that is off-limits to God?

Search the Scripture
- Read 2 Kings 4:1-2. Have you had a personal experience dealing with the death of a loved one? How did you react? Explain your feelings.
- When you look at your faith level now as compared to a year ago, are you stronger or weaker spiritually?
- Read Proverbs 18:10. Has God proven to you that He is a safe haven?
- Read Romans 9:28. In what way is God going to expedite your deliverance?

Chapter 11—No Fire in the House

Thoughts to Target
- What did Bishop Greenwood mean when he said, "One purpose of the Holy Spirit is to keep us consistent in our Christian walk"? Do you agree?
- How do you help someone to get back on track?
- Regarding the Seven Steps to Quality Devotions, how do you feel about being honest with God when dealing with your emotions?
- How do we express an attitude of gratitude towards God? When struggling with a lack of spiritual fire, how does Bishop

Greenwood tell you to re-light your passion for ministry?

• Does the Lord care if we are lukewarm? Explain. Is God our only true source of spiritual fire?

• How does Bishop Greenwood relate the fire of God to the anointing of the Spirit? Are they the same? Can you have one without the other?

Search the Scripture

• Read Psalm 27:1. Who is our true source of salvation?

• Read Acts 2:1-2. What does it mean to be full of the Holy Ghost? Why did Jesus command that we do this?

• Read John 15:26-27. What is the job of the Holy Spirit?

Chapter 12—God Is Our Rock

Thoughts to Target

• Do you agree with Bishop Greenwood that pastors need prayer and also need to pray?

• Has God always answered your requests to Him in a positive way? How did you feel when God said no, or gave no response?

• Have you found God to be your rock in times of trouble?

• How have you dealt with the Goliaths in your life?

• Read 2 Timothy. Is it comforting to know God has never been defeated?

• Read Ephesians 6:13. How do we put on the whole armor of God?

Thoughts to Target
• Whenever you've been down in spirit, how did God restore your confidence and security?
• Do you struggle with self-image? Explain.
• In the Bible, whom do you look to as a pattern of encouragement?
• How does God feel about your past? How do you feel about your future?
• David encouraged himself; how do you encourage yourself in the Lord?
• What lesson did you learn from Mr. Squirrel?
• Sometime I become so engrossed in the journey that I forget to enjoy the trip. How do you balance your ministry with the rest of your life? Explain your thoughts.
• Do you feel it is wrong to periodically take vacations from your ministry? What did Jesus mean when he said, "Rest awhile"?

Search the Scripture
• Read Matthew 4:11. How has God strengthened you from time to time?
• Read Psalm 24:7-10. What does the Lord ask you to do here?
• Bishop Greenwood said, "Feelings of remorse can engulf your spirit and fill you with regret as you rehearse the failures and faults of the past." How do you feel about this statement?
• Read Deuteronomy 11:12. How does it make you feel to know that you are never out of the sight of God? Explain.

POWERFUL DAILY CONFESSIONS

MAY THE BLESSINGS OF THE LORD BE UPON YOU!

I DESTROY EVERY CURSE OF FINANCIAL SETBACK IN MY FAMILY IN JESUS' NAME.

I PRAY FOR WITTY INVENTIONS THAT WILL RESULT IN DEBT CANCELLATION IN MY LIFE (PROV. 8:12).

I COMMAND EVERY PROBLEM THAT HAS RISEN AGAINST ME TO STOP AND TURN AROUND NOW, IN JESUS' NAME.

I PRAY FOR THE RESTORATION AND THE INCREASE OF THE MY FINANCES. LORD, I ASK FOR RESTORATION ACCORDING TO MATT 7:7.

I ASK YOU, LORD, TO MULTIPLY MY FINANCES AND GIVE ME FAVOR AND DIRECTION FROM YOUR WORD, ACCORDING TO LUKE 6:38.

I PRAY FOR WISDOM, KNOWLEDGE, AND BOLDNESS TO ADMINISTRATE IN THE MINISTRY OF THE LORD AS HE DIRECTS.

I ASK FOR WISDOM AND GOD'S PROTECTION FOR MY CHILDREN

I PRAY, LORD, GIVE ME THE RIGHT MENTORS TO MINISTER INTO MY LIFE AS LEADERS AND PASTORS.

I PRAY THAT THE LORD WILL BE GLORIFIED IN MY LIFE AND THROUGH MY LIVING.

I ASK FOR BLESSINGS ON MYSELF AS A HUSBAND/WIFE AND AS THE HEAD/SUPPORT OF MY HOME.

LORD, PLEASE GIVE ME WISDOM AND KNOWLEDGE AND LISTENING EARS FOR YOUR DIRECTION.

I PRAY THAT HEALING AND RESTORATION WILL TAKE PLACE IN ALL MY RELATIONSHIPS.

I PRAY THAT I BECOME THE MAN/WOMAN THAT JESUS CHRIST WOULD BE PLEASED IN, AND THAT I WOULD BE AN EXAMPLE IN WORD AND DEED. I COMMIT TO PRAYING MORE EACH DAY.

I ASK FOR DISCIPLINE IN THE THINGS THAT I SET MYSELF TO ACCOMPLISH IN THE MINISTRY AND IN EVERYDAY LIVING.

I ASK TO BECOME FINANCIALLY STABLE AND BECOME A BLESSING TO OTHERS ACCORDING TO DEUT. 8:18.

I COMMAND ALL MY FINANCES TO BE RELEASED IN JESUS' NAME.

I PRAY THAT HARVEST WOULD MEET HARVEST IN MY LIFE.

I DECLARE BY FAITH THE REST OF MY YEARS SHALL NOT BE ONES OF STRUGGLE BUT PROSPERITY.

I PRAY THAT DESPITE THE ATTACK OF THE ENEMY, I SHALL HAVE GOD'S PROMOTION AND FAVOR.

I RECEIVE THE CREATIVITY FOR THE CREATION OF WEALTH IN JESUS' NAME.

EVERY STEP I TAKE WILL RESULT IN BLESSINGS AND INCREASE IN JESUS' NAME.

I ASK FOR GOD'S BLESSINGS THAT WOULD MAKE ME A LENDER AND NOT A BORROWER.

ALL THIS I ASK IN JESUS' NAME. AMEN…

About the Author

Bishop R.E. Greenwood is the founder and senior pastor of HigherGround Christian Center, a multi-cultural ministry located in Douglasville, Georgia. HigherGround's purpose is to bring the un-churched into fellowship and membership through sharing the Gospel of Jesus Christ, to equip them for the work of their ministry, to develop disciples to maturity in Christ, and to teach them to celebrate God and magnify Him through worship.

Bishop Greenwood has ministered in many ecumenical conferences and crusades throughout North America, the United Kingdom, and France.

He has been married for more than 20 years to his wife Marion and they have two children, Christina and Darion.